AVRO
LANCASTER
LINCOLN AND
YORK

IN POST-WAR
RAF SERVICE
1945 – 1950

AVRO LANCASTER LINCOLN AND YORK

IN POST-WAR RAF SERVICE 1945 – 1950

Martin Derry

DALRYMPLE
& VERDUN

PUBLISHING

Avro Lancaster Lincoln and York
In Post-War RAF Service
1945 – 1950

Martin Derry

ISBN 978-1-905414-13-0

First published in 2010 by
Dalrymple & Verdun Publishing
33 Adelaide Street
Stamford PE9 2EN
United Kingdom
Tel: 0845 838 1940
mail@dvpublishing.co.uk
www.dvpublishing.co.uk

© Concept and design
Dalrymple & Verdun Publishing and
Stephen Thompson Associates
© Martin Derry 2010
© Richard Caruana

The right of Martin Derry to be
identified as the author of this work
has been asserted in accordance with
sections 77 and 78 of the Copyright
Designs and Patents Act, 1988.

Printed in England by
Ian Allan Printing Limited
Riverdene Business Park
Molesey Road
Horsham KT12 4RG

CONTENTS

Title page: Lancaster B.7(FE) NX612, wearing the code '9X-' of No.1689 (Ferry Pilot Training) Flight, flown by a pilot from No.20 MU during 1946. (See Wellington RP550, in 'Setting the Scene', for further information regarding No.1689 Flight and No.20 MU.) Viewed from this angle, NX612 reveals the stark simplicity of the FE colour scheme and the demarcation between the two colours. Following a period with the Austin Motor Company Ltd, NX612 was sold for scrap in February 1950. via Author

Opposite: Lancaster B.1(FE) PA414, 'MG-G' late of No.7 Squadron, High Street, Grantham, Lincolnshire. Built as a B.1 and subsequently modified to FE standard, PA414 served first with No.35 Squadron as 'TL-Q' from February 1946 until transferred to No.7 Squadron eight months later. This surely must have been the last place that any of Grantham's shoppers could have expected to see a Lancaster, which was, apparently, on its last journey, it having been SOC on 20th October 1948. However, might this photograph represent another earlier occasion - having been used as a static exhibit perhaps? Whatever the truth, not only are both turrets intact, they still have their .303in (dorsal) and .5in (rear) mgs mounted. Number 7 Squadron began receiving Lincoln B.2s in August 1949, although Lancasters remained on strength until January 1950.
Newark Air Museum

AUTHOR'S NOTES

1. It is not the author's intention to reproduce a further account of the Lancaster's development, wartime service and exploits so thoroughly examined and documented elsewhere. Rather, this volume is intended primarily to illustrate something of the Lancaster and its derivatives largely overlooked yet extensive post-war service. This is centred in the belief that a picture can be worth a thousand words, assisted by informative captions and background text. Also included is a précised account of the aircraft's genesis which might, conceivably, prove useful to a few readers. It is hoped therefore that this synthesis will provide an addition to the enthusiast's library, and add a little to their understanding of the Lancaster et al's post-war service.

2. B or not (to) B: At some point during the war the prefix 'B' began to appear in reference to the Lancaster and other RAF bombers: thus Lancaster marks I and III became the Lancaster B.I and B.III. For the sake of continuity (but excluding the Manchester), the designator B (Bomber) is used throughout where applicable.

3. Prior to June 1948, Roman numerals had been used to represent mark numbers. From June, these were replaced by Arabic numerals within Britain's armed forces: thus the Lincoln B.II for example became the B.2. For simplicity's sake, post-1945 reference to aircraft marks employ Arabic numerals irrespective of which side of the June 1948 divide they fall.

4. Other than for general references within the body of this work, space precludes incorporating a list of aircraft specifications. It is fully intended however to include such details in a following volume.

AUTHOR'S ACKNOWLEDGEMENTS

The author wishes to express his gratitude to Mike Smith - curator of the Newark Air Museum, for the use of his valuable time, knowledge and resources and for allowing access to the Museum's archive of photographs, very many of which appear in this volume. Grateful thanks are also extended to: Phil Butler, Tony Buttler, Richard Caruana, Joe L'Estrange, Jim Hughes, Roger Lindsay, Tony O'Toole, Simon Watson and Brandon White for the much appreciated contribution of their photographs. Additionally, I would like to thank my father Doug Derry for the countless hours he spent collating hundreds of photographs and negatives in preparation for this and other titles; Chris Salter for the invaluable contribution of both his subject and printing knowledge and finally to Steve Thompson for the book design.

Should any reader posess photographs that they feel ought to be included in future publications concerning British military aviation would they please contact the author via the publisher.

As World War II in Europe drew towards its conclusion in May 1945, jet-powered flight was an established fact, albeit as a mode of power still very much in its infancy. Today's casual observers would perhaps assume, if they even gave it a moment's thought, that the jet engine must have swept the piston engine from the skies within a half-dozen years or so of the war's end. And in any case, surely, wasn't the 1950s Korean war fought exclusively by jet-powered MiGs against something similar that the Americans had? Not quite! The truth is of course that following World War II's conclusion, piston-powered aircraft continued to ply their trade, in quantity, for another twenty years and more, before rapidly acquiescing to the evermore dominant, powerful and increasingly efficient jet engine.

In May 1945, Britain's Royal Air Force had fielded jet-powered Gloster Meteor fighters for almost a year and they would be joined by de Havilland Vampire jet fighters from 1946. However, in all other respects the RAF and its aircraft relied upon the piston engine.

At the War's end, Britain possessed a plethora of military equipment and down-sizing the armed forces to peace-time levels was essential, both as an economic measure and to release service personnel back into industry - if jobs could be found! In any event far-reaching savings had to be made. Financially the UK was in a parlous state and an age of even greater austerity loomed in a country where social and welfare issues demanded action from the new socialist government. Shockingly, at this time, over four million (of 12 million) homes still lacked hot water, baths and, in some areas, adequate sanitation. Unemployment rose from 400,000 to 1,750,000, yet, to combat absenteeism from the workplace it proved necessary to ban sport on weekdays. Effectively bankrupt, the British Government was ultimately forced by circumstances to commence negotiations with the USA in December 1945 for a loan of just over £1 billion, a colossal sum by contemporary standards that was to be repaid in 50 annual instalments from 1950 at a 2% rate of interest. (The final £42.5 million payment was made in December 2006 following several deferrals over the years.) The loan was conditional; it was not to be spent on the Labour government's welfare reforms, though whether or not any of it was is unclear.

Above: **Two unidentified Short Stirlings with Avro Ansons to the right of picture. It remains ironic that a clue to this aircraft's Achilles heel lay in the manufacturer's name; the wing was too short. Consequently the Stirling was unable to reach the higher operating altitudes achieved by its contemporaries, causing its withdrawal from the bombing offensive as sufficient Lancasters and Halifaxes became available. However, with nose and dorsal turrets removed, converted Stirling bombers were successfully used as glider-tugs and as transport aircraft from 1944. Some continued to serve for a short time into the post-war period** supplemented by purpose-built transport variants (Stirling V) until mid-1946, after which it would seem, other than any remaining in storage, the Stirling's RAF career ceased. As a postscript however, it is perhaps worth mentioning, that a small number of Stirling Vs were converted for civil use, with at least 10 being obtained by the Belgian company Trans-Air. Reportedly, five or six of these Stirlings were later acquired by the Royal Egyptian Air Force for operations against the new state of Israel with some surviving until 1950! Author's collection

Above: An unidentified Halifax A.IX. This variant was produced as a supply and troop-carrier for the airborne forces and, externally at least, other than lacking a dorsal turret its appearance was nearly identical to the radial-engined Halifaxes that had served with Bomber Command. Although that Command commenced a rapid withdrawal of Halifaxes from its order-of-battle in May 1945, Coastal Command continued to use the type on meteorological duties until as late as 1952. It would seem however that the last serviceable Halifax in RAF service was A.IX RT936 which was operated by the Parachute Training School until struck off charge following an accident in April 1953. The Halifax seen in this image is equipped with a Boulton Paul turret mounting two .5in machine guns, below which a glider towing attachment point is visible. Author's collection

So, where did this leave the subject of this book within the RAF following VE Day (Victory in Europe Day, 8th May 1945); an aircraft forever associated with RAF Bomber Command?

RAF Bomber Command had formed in 1936. In September 1939, following the opening of hostilities with Germany, the Command commenced its wartime campaign against Hitler's Third Reich and was equipped with the three twin-engined 'heavies' of the day: the Vickers Wellington, Handley Page Hampden and Armstrong Whitworth Whitley. These were later supplemented by larger and heavier 'heavies', name-ly: the Avro Manchester, Short Stirling, Handley Page Halifax and Avro Lancaster, the last three of which were all four-engined aircraft. Of the twin-engined types the Whitley, Hampden and Manchester were withdrawn from Bomber Command operations in 1942, followed by the Wellington in late 1943, whilst the four-engined Stirling soldiered on with Bomber Command in diminishing quantities until September 1944. Thereafter, the role of strategic bombing was left to the RAF's two outstanding four-engined bombers of the era: the Halifax (radial engined vari-ants) and Lancaster.

Halifax III (ex-B.III) LW385, 'L9-H' of No.190 Squadron, Transport Command seen post-May 1945. This aircraft had served as a bomber with Nos.431 and 434 Squadrons, Royal Canadian Air Force (RCAF) prior to joining No.190 Squadron, which disbanded at the end of 1945. LW385 was later allocated to the Royal Aircraft Establishment (RAE) and was SOC on 12th March 1948. Author's collection

However, as the war in Europe neared its end the decision was made to scale down Bomber Command which would operate only one type of four-engined bomber following VE Day, supplemented by later designs as they became available; thus was the Lancaster retained. On 7th May 1945 the axe fell upon the Command's Halifaxes when all 11 squadrons of No.4 Group were transferred to Transport Command. Any remaining Halifax units within the Command rapidly disposed of their aircraft which were then allocated elsewhere, stored, sold or scrapped; in any event its days as an RAF bomber were finished. With the war against the Japanese still continuing it was envisaged that Britain would deploy as many resources as it was able against Japan, including tropicalised Lancasters. With the dropping of the two atomic bombs on Japan in August 1945 however, such deployments proved unnecessary.

For the Lancaster, as stated, a future still beckoned with Bomber Command and, additionally, with Coastal Command too as well as a miscellany of other RAF units, foreign air forces and as test-beds for future aircraft power-plants and systems. Moreover, a new Lancaster variant would undergo a metamorphosis to emerge as the Lincoln, which would prove to be the last piston-engined strategic bomber to serve the RAF, outliving as it did the more sophisticated Boeing Washington B.1 (*née* B.29 Superfortress) within Bomber Command.

Below: **A poor quality image showing Wellington T.10, 'FM-AA', belonging to No.201 AFS in 1948/49. Although unidentified this might possibly be NA849 which did serve with this unit and carried the unit code and individual code shown here. Until 1951, No.201 AFS's identifying codes were 'FMA' and 'FMB'; the aircraft's individual code being, in this instance, 'A'. Assuming that this aircraft is Wellington NA849, it was sold for scrap on 30th December 1953.** Author's collection

Above: **In terms of bombers, other than Avro's Lancaster (plus, if pedantic, the Avro Anson also), the RAF's other great survivor from WWII was the Wellington, albeit redirected towards training roles rather than offensive. Nevertheless, its continuing utility was not to be denied and the Wellington 10 and T.10 continued to serve into the 1950s. Ultimately, it was T.10, MF628 which made the last flight of any Wellington on 24th January 1955, when it was flown to the Vickers airfield at Wisley, Surrey for eventual preservation. This undated image shows Wellington 10, RP550 coded '9X-S'. Records imply that this aircraft served only with No.202 Advanced Flying School (AFS) followed by No.201 AFS. However, the code 9X was allocated to No.1689 (Ferry Pilot Training) Flight, within No.20 Maintenance Unit (MU) at Aston Down, Gloucestershire, which operated a fleet of aircraft including Wellingtons, Lancasters and Lincolns. RP550 was not converted into a T.10 and was struck off charge (SOC) in January 1950, while No.1689 Flight survived until disbanded in April 1953, when it was absorbed by the Ferry Training Unit at Benson, Oxfordshire.** Author's collection

A BRIEF INTRODUCTION TO THE LANCASTER

The Lancaster was derived from the Avro 679 Manchester bomber powered by two Rolls-Royce 24 cylinder Vulture engines each designed to develop a little under 1800 horse power. The prototype Manchester, L7246, flew for the first time on 25th July 1939 and problems emerged from the outset. Essentially both engines ran very hot and were unable to develop their projected power output; a portent of the future! They however were perhaps less of a problem at such an early stage than those experienced with the airframe. The Manchester had been conceived with a wingspan of just 72' which was considered marginal even in the design stage, so by the time L7246 first flew the span had been increased to 80ft-2in, (some sources state 82ft-2in). Even so, the first flight indicated the need for a further major increase in span which would eventually be finalised at 90ft-1in. The aircraft also suffered from a lack of directional stability caused by an underestimation of the size of tail fin area required; this was remedied by increasing the number of tail fins from two to three. In this form the Manchester I entered RAF squadron service with No.207 Squadron which reformed on November 1st 1940, receiving its first Manchester a few days later. Further airframe improvements would follow as Manchester development and service experience revealed additional problems, solutions to which would be incorporated on the production line. Two improvements in particular were listed:

a) Increase the span of the tail plane by 5ft to 33ft, albeit still mounting the three fins. (Surviving Manchester Is already fitted and delivered with 28ft span tail planes [or 22ft, again sources conflict], numbering 20 originally were to have replacement 33ft tail planes fitted retrospectively in late 1942. Presumably, if correct and given the Manchester's poor reputation by 1942, that aspect of the programme was never commenced!)

b) Incorporate at a later stage, significantly larger tail fins and rudders thus allowing the third fin to be dispensed with. Manchesters delivered with the twin-fin 33ft tail plane were (semi-officially) designated Manchester IA. This installation was fitted to at least 27 Manchesters on the production line and retrospectively to a number of Mk.Is which thus became Mk.IAs.

With the Manchester IA, there can be little doubt that the airframe had matured considerably, achieving something of the proportional look of the later Lancaster, albeit with only two engines and a 'wrong shape' dorsal turret. So what went amiss for this aircraft? In short, the Vulture engines proved to be unreliable, under-powered and thus unsuited to the demands of war, despite the best efforts of Rolls-Royce engineers to overcome the engines' problems - problems exacerbated by the incremental increase in weight of the aircraft. Consequently, Manchester production was limited to just 200 machines (plus two prototypes), and the surviving aircraft were withdrawn from operational service, its final bombing operations occurring in late June 1942. Beyond this date, some survivors continued to serve with training units until the second half of 1943.

Being aware of the Air Ministry's future requirements in respect of strategic bombers, Avro's chief designer, Roy Chadwick, had long-considered potential developments of the Manchester I and its basic airframe, an airframe which was already recognised as possessing both sound qualities and, significantly, a large uninterrupted bomb bay. This train of thought

Manchester IA believed to be L7320. This aircraft was involved in a number of publicity photographs all of which had the serial number erased by the censor, and several of which revealed that the starboard undercarriage doors had failed to close properly during this flight. This Manchester was built as a Mk.I, so if indeed this really is L7320 there appears to be no mention in its record of having been converted to a Mk.IA. Newark Air Museum

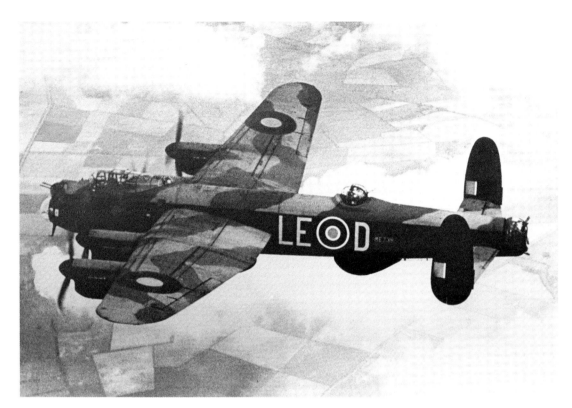

Above: An undated photograph of Lancaster B.I ME739, 'LE-D' of No.630 Squadron. This photograph portrays the classic wartime image of a Lancaster, irrespective of whether it was a B.I or B.III - the principal variants operated by Bomber Command during the war years. Both marks were virtually identical save for the engines each employed; the B.I used Rolls-Royce Merlins whilst the B.III used American Packard Motors-built variants. Based at East Kirkby, Lincolnshire, ME739 was lost on the night of 10/11th April 1945, whilst attacking Leipzig; one crew member was killed, four were taken prisoner and two evaded capture. *Brandon White collection*

Below: Sporting a tally of 10 offensive sorties plus a hideous caricature of a bomb-toting toddler, ground crew are presumably preparing this unidentified Lancaster for its eleventh. This is unlikely to be a 'staged' image given that one of the ground crew is 'at ease' on the incendiary containers in the foreground, let alone the individual attending to something necessary at the aircraft's starboard wheel! *Newark Air Museum*

A Lancaster B.I being test flown by Alex Henshaw. Famously associated with the flight testing of Spitfires, he also test-flew Lancasters built at Castle Bromwich.
Newark Air Museum

preceded deliveries of the Manchester and preceded several of the serious technical problems later encountered too. One particular line of development that emerged, others notwithstanding, offered considerable potential by virtue of an increased wingspan able to accommodate four engines. Developed further, this four-engined concept was initially referred to as the Manchester III, although an alternative term 'Lancaster' was certainly in common usage at Avro by December 1940, and as early as mid-1940 by their design staff, and possibly earlier still. In essence, the four-engined aircraft had been envisaged well before the Manchester I entered into squadron service and in fact Avro were ready to progress with a prototype Type 683 'Lancaster' by late 1940. Avro were instructed to proceed with the construction of the prototype and, in order to expedite its production, the company removed a Manchester I from the production line complete with triple-tail and small span tail-plane. Its two Vulture engines were replaced by four Rolls-Royce Merlins. For security purposes however, Avro were required to cease using the term Lancaster temporarily, substituting it for Manchester III instead. The prototype 683, serial number BT308, first flew on 9th January 1941, just six weeks after work on it had commenced, and even that short period of time included almost a week's delay caused by adverse weather conditions during early January.

Sources conflict as to whether or not BT308 was still officially known as a Manchester III when first flown or a Lancaster. Ultimately of course the name Lancaster was officially adopted and was a wise decision, one that doubtlessly disassociated as far as possible the Lancaster from its much troubled forebear as its problems became ever more manifest during 1941.

The Lancaster proved to be successful from the outset, with its place in history as assured as that of Bomber Command's air and ground crews. Having entered into the Command's inventory, the bomber's operational career commenced in the late evening of 3rd March 1942, when just four of its type conducted a minelaying operation in German waters. By late 1943, it was frequently possible to dispatch to Berlin over 400 Lancasters in one night and, by February 1945, double that number could be summoned if required. Lancasters completed their final bombing missions against the Third Reich on 25th April 1945, having completed something in excess of 152,000 operational sorties. This resulted in a loss caused by enemy action of approximately 3,460 of their number, from a total production figure of 7,377 covering all marks, three prototypes and includes those Lancasters delivered in 1946 when production ceased. Additionally, many others were lost in wartime accidents or were written-off having received extensive battle-damage, yet succeeded in returning to a friendly base.

Opposite bottom: **A close-up study of an unidentified Lancaster B.II's Hercules starboard engines and propellers. The white plaques on the engine nacelles simply state 'OIL DTD 472'.** Newark Air Museum

Above: Lancaster B.II DS689, 'OW-S' of No.426 Squadron Royal Canadian Air Force in 1943. The B.II was immediately identifiable from all other Lancaster marks by virtue of its Bristol Hercules radial engines, introduced to the Lancaster as an insurance against a possible shortage of Merlins. In the event, the shortage never transpired and only 300 production B.IIs were built, very few of which survived the war, and those that did existed mostly with conversion units. The longest lived B.IIs were probably LL735 and LL736 in use as trials aircraft until March and June 1950 respectively. As for DS689, it was brought down during a raid against Stuttgart on 7/8th October 1943; six of the crew were killed and two evaded capture.
Author's collection

1.

THE BOMBERS

Following VE Day, the Allies need was to defeat Japan; meaning air and sea bombardment followed by a ground-assault of the Japanese mainland and acceptance of the appalling casualty list, both Allied and Japanese, thus implied. From Britain's perspective significant air, ground and sea assets were already deployed in the Far East, but more was now required. The aerial element of these additional forces was to be met by the deployment of *Tiger Force*, a balanced air force comprising British and Commonwealth units containing bombers (Lancasters), fighters (Hawker Tempest IIs, de Havilland Mosquitos and, later, de Havilland Hornet Is), plus transport and other aircraft. The Lancaster force would comprise modified and tropicalised Lancaster B.Is and B.VIIs which, so modified, acquired the suffix FE (Far East) to become B.I(FE) and B.VII(FE) respectively. With the war expected to extend well into 1946 and probably beyond, it was intended that the Lincoln with its greater fuel capacity and range would supplement the Lancasters as soon as possible, however, as stated earlier Japan capitulated following the atomic bomb attacks of August 1945,

and the invasion of mainland Japan was thus avoided. As a consequence, *Tiger Force* was laid to rest on 31st October 1945.

Although matters would soon change, VE Day found Bomber Command fielding both a surplus of, and several marks of Lancaster, principally composed of B.Is, B.IIIs, B.VIIs and Canadian-built B.Xs in addition to the FE variants as they became available. The B.X equipped seven squadrons within the Command's No.6 Group (RCAF) by war's end, all of which were redeployed to Canada from June 1945 in order to prepare for *Tiger Force*. Remaining UK based Canadian units in No.6 Group equipped with Lancaster B.Is and B.IIIs, remained with the RAF, for the time being, and were transferred to No.1 Group prior to No.6 Groups's disbandment on 31st August 1945. They, and many other Lancaster squadrons, became heavily involved in ferrying troops to and from the UK, and ferrying ex-POWs home.

Following their signing of the surrender document in Tokyo Bay on 2nd September 1945, and the demise of *Tiger Force* a few weeks later, the RAF's requirement for heavy bombers was

Above: Lancaster B.7(FE) NX678, 'WS-S' of No.9 Squadron, displaying their Squadron Motif: a bat, their motto being 'Throughout the night we fly'. Lancaster B.7(FE)s began to arrive with this unit from late-1945, a little prior to the deployment of both Nos.9 and 617 Squadrons to Salbani, India in January 1946, for a four month deployment. Their purpose was to assist India's transition towards independence and to help deter any likelihood of aggression towards departing British forces. Additionally, they participated in a fly-past over Delhi and were on hand should a reported mutiny by elements of the Royal Indian Navy develop further; it didn't. Having returned to the UK, No.9 Squadron

began its transition to Lincolns in July 1946 and bade farewell to its Lancasters shortly thereafter. NX678 seems only to have served with this Squadron, but was not scrapped until 1955. NX678 was one of 180 B.7s completed, of which 150 were delivered in serial ranges: NX611-NX648, NX661-NX703, NX715-NX758 and NX770-NX794; the final 30 received serial numbers RT670-RT699. If not all, then certainly the great majority of B.7s were delivered as B.7(FE)s and, following delivery, large numbers of them languished in storage until scrapped or, for some, were allocated to France in the 1950s. via Roger Lindsay

Above: **Lancaster B.1(Special) PD131, 'LS-V' No.15 Squadron, 1946.** First issued to No.617 Squadron as 'YZ-A', this Lancaster was one of six which dropped 'Grand Slam' (22,000lb) bombs onto the Arnsberg railway viaduct on 19th March 1945, resulting in a 40-foot breach of the structure. On 25th April it participated in an attack against Hitler's Berchtesgaten, dropping a 'Tallboy' (12,000lb) bomb. Thereafter, PD131 was allocated to No.15 Squadron and was employed during 1946 in Operation *Front Line*. This operation involved the dropping of 'Grand Slam' and 'Tallboy' deep penetration bombs in conjunction with US B-29 Superfortresses, onto the heavily reinforced U-boat pens at Farge, near Bremen, Germany. PD131 was SOC on 19th May 1947, whilst No.15 Squadron re-equipped with Lincoln B.2s from February 1947, followed by B.29 Washingtons from January 1951. Newark Air Museum

reassessed based upon peacetime factors and its then current commitments. Bomber Command would slim down drastically and lose Nos.5, 6 and 8 Groups by the end of 1945, having already lost Nos.4 and 6 as previously related, but operationally its structure, form and function would remain recognisably the same albeit comprised of just Nos.1 and 3 Groups. When Bomber Command's needs were assessed in conjunction with those of the RAF in the Middle and Far East, the total quantity of heavy bombers deemed necessary was, broadly speaking, 445 Lancasters. This quantity was intended to allow for the replacement of American-built Consolidated Liberator B-24, four-engined bombers operated by the RAF in the Middle and Far East, which would soon have to be returned to US control as stipulated by the terms of the wartime Lend-Lease Act of March 1941. FE standard Lancasters were considered apt replacements for service in those regions, whilst standard Lancasters would suffice at home. The figure of 445 however was not to be realised and was soon reduced to approximately 270. These two quantities it ought to be said, are uncorroborated, but if correct the figure of 270 would presumably refer to the front-line operational strength, include Lincolns – but exclude reserves. Given that Bomber Command would reduce to 22 heavy bomber squadrons during 1946, and including four further squadrons based in the Middle East, that would allow an average complement of just over 10 aircraft per unit. It is known that several squadrons operated at a peacetime establishment of just eight aircraft each for a time, (equivalent to a wartime Flight), although others received more, No.35 Squadron for instance despatched 16 Lancasters on its goodwill tour of the USA in 1946. Perhaps therefore, in 1946, the figure of 270 was valid?

This image is apparently that of a crater made by a 'Tallboy' (12,000lb) deep penetration bomb dropped on Heligoland during post-war bombing trials. The author cannot vouch for the veracity of either statement, but the four people on the far-side of the crater lend scale to a very a large hole! Certainly the (forcibly) uninhabited island which lies some 300 miles east of the Humber Estuary, was used by the RAF until 1952 as a bombing range, so the information supplied with the image is, conceivably, correct. Newark Air Museum

Ultimately, given the state of Britain's finances plus a declining empire, the reduction was not perhaps as grievous as at first it might appear, given Britain's resolve to withdraw from India. It meant that the need for permanently based heavy bombers in that portion of the globe would be diminished, any such requirements could be met by temporary (yet often lengthy) deployments from Bomber Command, as distinct from the several post-war short-term exercises in which its bombers would participate. The Middle East however was another matter. The Suez Canal – imperative to Britain's Merchant Navy and hence trade and commerce, was seen as a particularly vulnerable choke point which had to be protected; other forces notwithstanding, the RAF would maintain at least four Lancaster bomber squadrons in the region – for the time being at least.

Until Lincolns entered service, RAF heavy bomber units were to be equipped primarily with Lancaster B.I and B.VII variants and would steadily relinquish the Packard Merlin-powered B.III. This was to ensure that their aircraft were fitted with Rolls-Royce Merlins as an insurance against any possible disruption of supply from the USA. Further, with Lancaster production still continuing in late-1945, and with a large surplus available, it was decided that, for Bomber Command at least, Lancasters with more than 150 hours flying time 'on the clock' would be replaced. As a legacy of *Tiger Force*, now-surplus Lancaster B.1(FE)s and B.VII(FE)s began arriving at RAF units from late-1945 and, ultimately, equipped most of Bomber Command's surviving Lancaster squadrons too. The FE variants were distinctively painted white overall with black undersides and were equipped with dorsal turrets, which otherwise, were to have been (or had been) removed to compensate for the additional bomb bay fuel tanks required for operations over the Pacific for which they were originally envisaged.

A curiosity with the Lancaster, as distinct from many other warplane types, was that the principal production variants: B.I, B.III, B.VII and B.X, in terms of major components, were all essentially the same. The increase in mark number did not indicate any particular increase in capability in terms of overall performance, whereas, for example, Supermarine's Spitfire F.XIV represented a very real increase in capability over the Mk.I or V. In fact, the last Lancasters to be delivered, in March 1946, were B.Is! Differences did exist of course, perhaps the least obvious being whether or not Rolls-Royce or Packard-built engines were fitted and of what mark. More obvious, externally at least, was the shape and position of the dorsal turret. The B.VII was fitted with a dorsal turret sited further forward along the fuselage than other marks; manufactured by the American Glenn Martin Company, it mounted twin-Browning .5in machine-guns (mgs), and didn't require a fairing. The others marks all featured twin-Browning .303in mgs in dorsal turrets which did employ a most distinct fairing. Both the B.I(FE) and B.VII(FE) received Fraser Nash FN82 rear turrets equipped with twin .5in mgs, while surviving B.IIIs converted to become ASR.IIIs or GR.IIIs lost their dorsal turrets but retained four Browning .303in mgs in the tail. (The latter two marks also had distinctive vision panels fitted in the fuselage forward of the tailplane). Such distinctions of course only lasted whilst each Lancaster retained a dorsal turret or indeed, mounted any guns at all, in which case, to the uninitiated, they might all equally be described as 'Mark Is'. An appropriate illustration of this is provided by the B.VII, of which 180 were built and delivered between April 1945 and January 1946. However, 50 others had been constructed earlier, but following a delay in the receipt of their Martin dorsal turrets each consequently received, in lieu, Fraser Nash turrets mounting twin .303in mgs – as fitted to the other marks – and consequently all 50 were simply redesignated as B.Is and delivered as such from February to April 1945. (Occasionally the reader may find these 50 Lancasters: serial numbers NX548-NX589 and NX603-NX610, listed as B.VII 'Interim'.)

Opposite top left, right, centre left and right: **Lancaster B.1(FE)s of No.35 (Madras Presidency) Squadron. During the first quarter of 1946, the concept of a goodwill tour of the USA by a Bomber Command squadron was considered and then developed to become, appropriately enough, Operation *Goodwill*. Number 35 Squadron was chosen to undertake the six-week tour of the USA which would comprise 16 Lancaster B.1(FE)s. They departed their base at Gravely, Cambridgeshire, on 9th July 1946, flying via the Azores, Gander, Newfoundland, and on to the USA. The images shown here were taken on 1st August 1946, during the US Army Air Force Day celebrations at Long Beach Field, Los Angeles. The 16 Lancasters were accompanied by a supporting Avro York which is visible to the rear of one of the images, from amongst which, Lancasters PA385 'S', TW657 'C' and TW878 'H' can be distinguished. Even further to the rear, on the far-side of the airfield, a collection of North American T.6s, Douglas C-47s, Curtiss C-46s and a solitary Lockheed P-38 Lightning can be identified.** Newark Air Museum

Opposite bottom: **Lancaster B.1(FE) TW879, 'TL-E' of No.35 Squadron seen whilst participating in the tour of the USA. Just visible below the cockpit and just ahead of the leading edge of the starboard wing, is the Squadron's Motif which bears the head of a winged horse, commemorating the units co-operation with the cavalry in WWI. Apparently the Motif, which appeared on both sides of the cockpit, was applied just before their departure to the USA. TW879 was SOC on 19th November 1947, although the Squadron retained Lancasters until September 1949, having commenced its re-equipment with Lincolns a month earlier. The unit disbanded in February 1950 but reformed in September 1951, equipped with Washingtons.** via Tony O'Toole

BOMBER COMMAND'S
POST-WAR ORDERS OF BATTLE

In order to make any useful comparison between wartime and peacetime equipment levels, it is necessary first to appreciate the strength of the Command prior to VE Day. As of mid-April 1945, Bomber Command possessed a strength of some 1850 heavy bombers. Of this number, 475 or so were Halifaxes while the remainder was comprised of Lancaster B.Is, B.IIIs and B.Xs, although not all were serviceable at any one time. These aircraft were distributed amongst approximately 73 operational (or almost operational) squadrons, and takes no account of such aircraft awaiting collection from manufacturers, held with training units, conversion or maintenance units etc, or, in the Halifax's case with other Commands.

Nine months later, other than indicating the ongoing process of reduction towards its peacetime limit, Bomber Command's Order of Battle at the beginning of January 1946 also reflects the arrival of the first of the FE standard Lancasters and Lincoln B.2s at squadron level. Their arrival would cause a steady flow of Lancaster B.1s and B.3s to be sent to maintenance units (MU) during 1946, for storage or scrapping as the year progressed.

For the sake of brevity, changes made to Bomber Command's complement of squadrons, locations and aircraft types from 1946 are best conveyed in tabular form.

JANUARY 1946

NO.1 GROUP

Binbrook, Lincolnshire

| No.12 Sqn | Lancaster B.1 & B.3 | Sqn code | PH | |
| No.101 Sqn | Lancaster B.1 & B.3 | Sqn code | SR | |

Coningsby, Lincolnshire

| No.83 Sqn | Lancaster B.1 & B.3 | Sqn code | OL | |
| No.97 Sqn | Lancaster B.1 & B.3 | Sqn code | OF | |

Faldingworth, Lincolnshire

| No.300 Sqn | Lancaster B.1 & B.3 | Sqn code | BH | Polish unit, disbanded 11/10/46 |

Metheringham, Lincolnshire

| No.106 Sqn | Lancaster B.1 & B.3 | Sqn code | ZN | Disbanded 18/2/46 |

Scampton, Lincolnshire

| No.57 Sqn | Lancaster B.1 & B.3 & Lincoln B.2 | Sqn code | DX | |
| No.100 Sqn | Lancaster B.1 & B.3 | Sqn code | HW | |

Sturgate, Lincolnshire

| No.50 Sqn | Lancaster B.1 & B.3 | Sqn code | VN | |
| No.61 Sqn | Lancaster B.1 & B.3 | Sqn code | QR | |

Waddington, Lincolnshire

| No.9 Sqn | Lancaster B.7(FE) | Sqn code | WS | Both units deployed to Salbani, India |
| No.617 Sqn | Lancaster B.7(FE) | Sqn code | KC | from 1/1946 to 5/1946 |

Leeming, Yorkshire

| No.427 (Lion) Sqn | Lancaster B.1 & B.3 | Sqn code | ZL | Both were RCAF units which disbanded on 31/05/46 |
| No.429 (Bison) Sqn | Lancaster B.1 & B.3 | Sqn code | AL | |

NO.3 GROUP

Gravely, Cambridgeshire

No.35 Sqn	Lancaster B.1 & B.3	Sqn code	TL	
No.115 Sqn	Lancaster B.1 & B.3	Sqn code	KO	

Mildenhall, Suffolk

No.15 Sqn	Lancaster B.1 & B.3	Sqn code	LS	Also received a few B.1(Specials) for carriage of 22,000lb 'Grand Slam bomb
No.44 Sqn	Lancaster B.1 & B.3/ Lincoln B.2	Sqn code	KM	

Methwold, Norfolk

No.149 Sqn	Lancaster B.1 & B.3	Sqn code	OJ	
No.207 Sqn	Lancaster B.1 & B.3	Sqn code	EM	

Tuddenham, Suffolk

No.90 Sqn	Lancaster B.1 & B.3	Sqn code	WP	
No.138 Sqn	Lancaster B.1 & B.3	Sqn code	AC	(Sqn code changed to NF from December 46. It was certainly applied to B.1(FE)s)

Mepal, Cambridgeshire

No.7 Sqn	Lancaster B.1 & B.3	Sqn code	MG	
No.49 Sqn	Lancaster B.1 & B.3	Sqn code	EA	

Notes: *Additionally, No.75 (New Zealand) Sqn operated Lincolns at Spilsby, Lincolnshire, from September to 15th October 1945, on which date the unit was disbanded. Their Squadron code was 'AA'.*

Not part of Bomber Command, but included here for reference is No.205 (Heavy Bomber) Group which, in 1946, operated the following Lancaster equipped squadrons in defence of the Canal Zone:

No.40 Sqn Lancaster B.7(FE)s were received during 1/46. Squadron disbanded on 1/4/47.

No.104 Sqn Transferred from Italy to Egypt in 10/1945, received Lancaster B.7(FE)s soon after. Disbanded on 1/4/47.

No.178 Sqn Liberators replaced by Lancaster B.3s in late 1945. Squadron operated until renumbered as No.70 Sqn on 15/4/46, thereafter receiving a few B.1(FE)s. No.70 Sqn disbanded on 1/4/47.

No.214 Sqn Lancasters replaced Liberators in late 1945. Squadron operated until renumbered No.37 Sqn on 15/4/1946. (No.214 Sqn reformed as a UK-based bomber squadron during 11/46). No.37 Sqn operated Lancaster B.3s until re-equipped with B.7(FE)s from mid-1946. No.37 Sqn disbanded on 1/4/1947. (It re-emerged in 9/47, as a maritime squadron equipped with Lancaster GR.3s).

No.205 (Heavy Bomber) Group was disbanded on 31st March 1947.

JANUARY 1947

NO.1 GROUP

Binbrook, Lincolnshire

No.9 Sqn	Lincoln B.2	Sqn code	WS	Relocation commenced during April 46
No.12 Sqn	Lincoln B.2	Sqn code	PH	
No.101 Sqn	Lincoln B.2	Sqn code	SR	
No.617 Sqn	Lincoln B.2	Sqn code	KC	Relocated in May 46

Hemswell, Lincolnshire

No.83 Sqn	Lincoln B.2	Sqn code	OL	Relocated in October 46
No.97 Sqn	Lincoln B.2	Sqn code	OF	Relocated in November 46
No.100 Sqn	Lincoln B.2	Sqn code	HW	Relocated in October 46

Waddington, Lincolnshire

No.50 Sqn	Lincoln B.2	Sqn code	VN	Relocated in January 46
No.57 Sqn	Lincoln B.2	Sqn code	DX	Relocated in October 46
No.61 Sqn	Lincoln B.2	Sqn code	QR	Relocated in January 46

NO.3 GROUP

Stradishall, Suffolk

No.35 Sqn	Lancaster B.1(FE)	Sqn code	TL	Relocated in September 46
No.115 Sqn	Lancaster B.1(FE)	Sqn code	KO	Relocated in September 46
No.149 Sqn	Lancaster B.1(FE)	Sqn code	OJ	Relocated in November 46
No.207 Sqn	Lancaster B.1(FE)	Sqn code	EM	Relocated in November 46

Upwood, Huntingdonshire

No.7 Sqn	Lancaster B.1(FE)	Sqn code	MG	Relocated in July 46
No.49 Sqn	Lancaster B.1(FE)	Sqn code	EA	Relocated in July 46
No.148 Sqn	Lancaster B.1(FE)	Sqn code	AU	Reformed 4th November 46 at Upwood
No.214 Sqn	Lancaster B.1(FE)	Sqn code	QN	Reformed 4th November 46 at Upwood

Wyton, Huntingdonshire

No.15 Sqn	Lancaster B.1(FE)	Sqn code	LS	Relocated in August 46
No.44 Sqn	Lancaster B.1(FE)/ Lincoln B.2	Sqn code	KM	Relocated in August 46
No.90 Sqn	Lancaster B.1(FE)	Sqn code	WP	Relocated in August 46
No.138 Sqn	Lancaster B.1(FE)	Sqn code	NF	Relocated in November 46

The years 1948 and 1949 showed only small variations in comparison to the previous two. Both Groups remained static regarding their component squadrons and reasonably so with regard to their permanent bases; any variations were generally as a result of temporary deployments and operational or training exercises etc. The principal changes concerned the ongoing replacement of Lancasters by Lincolns.

1ST JANUARY 1950

NO.1 GROUP

Binbrook, Lincolnshire

No.9 Sqn	Lincoln B.2	Sqn code	WS	
No.12 Sqn	Lincoln B.2	Sqn code	PH	
No.101 Sqn	Lincoln B.2	Sqn code	SR	
No.617 Sqn	Lincoln B.2	Sqn code	KC	

Hemswell, Lincolnshire

No.83 Sqn	Lincoln B.2	Sqn code	OL	
No.97 Sqn	Lincoln B.2	Sqn code	OF	
No.100 Sqn	Lincoln B.2	Sqn code	HW	

Waddington, Lincolnshire

No.50 Sqn	Lincoln B.2	Sqn code	VN
No.57 Sqn	Lincoln B.2	Sqn code	DX
No.61 Sqn	Lincoln B.2	Sqn code	QR

NO.3 GROUP

Mildenhall, Suffolk

No.35 Sqn	Lincoln B.2	Sqn code	TL	
No.115 Sqn	Lancaster B.1(FE)/ Lincoln B.2	Sqn code	KO	Last Lancasters gone by end of 1/1950)
No.149 Sqn	Lincoln B.2	Sqn code	OJ	
No.207 Sqn	Lincoln B.2	Sqn code	EM	

All four of the above relocated to Mildenhall in February 1949. Other than No.115 Squadron, the other three units had replaced their Lancasters between August and November 1949.

Upwood, Huntingdonshire

No.7 Sqn	Lancaster B.1(FE)/ Lincoln B.2	Sqn code	MG	Last Lancasters gone by end of 1/1950)
No.49 Sqn	Lancaster B.1(FE)/ Lincoln B.2	Sqn code	EA	Last Lancasters gone by end of 3/1950)
No.148 Sqn	Lancaster B.1(FE)/ Lincoln B.2	Sqn code	AU	(Last Lancasters gone by end of 2/1950)
No.214 Sqn	Lancaster B.1(FE)/ Lincoln B.2	Sqn code	QN	(Last Lancasters gone by end of 2/1950)

Wyton, Huntingdonshire

No.15 Sqn	Lincoln B.2	Sqn code	LS
No.44 Sqn	Lincoln B.2	Sqn code	KM
No.90 Sqn	Lincoln B.2	Sqn code	WP
No.138 Sqn	Lincoln B.2	Sqn code	NF

Numbers 15 and 44 Squadron Lancasters were replaced during the first quarter of 1947, and Nos.90 and 138 Squadron Lancasters were replaced during the third quarter of 1947.

As can be seen, the Command's Lancasters were already in the process of being replaced by the Lincoln in 1946, a process largely completed by late-1949. Although Lancasters still lingered with the Upwood Wing into early 1950, few of those, if any, survived beyond March 1950. The mantle of strategic bomber within the RAF passed solely to the Lincoln until the first B-29 Washingtons entered service with No.149 Squadron in November 1950. (As a footnote, Bomber Command continued to be responsible for small quantities of photographic reconnaissance Lancaster PR.1s beyond 1950, - see section 2 'Other Units'.)

The Avro Lincoln was originally promulgated as the Lancaster B.IV and B.V as both were considered to be improved Lancasters featuring an increase in size, power and armament. An order for a prototype was placed in July 1943. It has been suggested that Lincolns possessed some 70% commonality with Lancasters! Whatever the true percentage and despite any obvious and understandable desire to retain the name of a successful and famous bomber, the remaining differences would have been more than sufficient to have created a logistical nightmare when supplying spares and materials to Lancaster units in general. A new name would distinguish the one from the other. Therefore sentiment was stood to one side, practicality was observed and the Lancaster B.IV and B.V became the Lincoln B.I and B.II respectively. Given the location of that City, the new name proved particularly apt. Large scale production orders for the two marks were placed, but most of these were cancelled as WWII was brought to its abrupt conclusion.

Ultimately, excluding those built abroad or for export, just 532 Lincolns were completed: 3 prototypes, 82 B.1s and 447 B.2s, while approximately 3700 were cancelled. Few sources agree as to what extent B.1s were ever used beyond conducting limited trials in 1945/46; certainly most were never employed and were flown to MUs for (outdoor) storage and were ultimately condemned having been declared obsolete in February 1949. However a few continued to find employment, one of them, RE232, in use with the Aircraft & Armament Experimental Establishment

(A&AEE) at Boscombe Down, Wiltshire, came to grief as late as 14th April 1950, when its undercarriage collapsed during takeoff at Silloth, Cumberland.

Only the B.2 variant equipped Bomber Command and the wider RAF. In comparison to the Lancaster the Lincoln's wingspan was increased by 18ft to 120ft and the fuselage length increased from 69ft-6ins to 78ft-3½in. Packard Merlin 68 engines were fitted, each rated at 1,750hp as compared to the (approximately) 1,020hp produced by those Merlins fitted to late-edition Lancasters. The Lincoln's defences were markedly improved by the installation of twin .5in mgs located in both the front and rear turrets, these were reinforced by twin-20mm cannon in the dorsal position; although explored, no ventral defence was provided.

As regards aircraft performance, describing the performance of any single type in general terms is often problematic, but drawing comparisons between the Lincoln and Lancaster, like-for-like, is fraught with ambiguity – suffice it to say that the Lincoln, as intended, was an improvement upon the Lancaster. Offensively, and ignoring the need to adapt an aircraft, both types were capable of lifting a 20,000lb + bomb load, although 14,000lb was a Lincoln's normal maximum subject to the amount of fuel to be carried, the total volume of which was, by virtue of its increased span, greater than that of the Lancaster. With a 14,000lb bomb load a range of 2,800 miles was possible, while a wartime Lancaster could generally achieve a range of 1,700 miles with a 12,000lb load. Dependant upon loads carried and other factors, the Lincolns' service ceiling was c 28,000ft with a maximum speed of 305mph at 19,000ft; more relevant than top speed was the cruising speed which reached 260mph at approximately 20,000ft, reducing to 244mph at 22,500ft. Lancasters could cruise at approximately 220mph at 20,000ft, which was about 3,000ft below their service ceiling but the latter's figures, let it be noted, varied as the war progressed primarily as more powerful engines became available.

Excluding No.75 Squadron, which had disbanded on 15th October 1945, twenty-two Bomber Command squadrons operated the Lincoln in its intended role as a bomber (see Order of Battle January 1950). No sooner had the Lancaster finally been replaced in the Upwood Wing, than the first Lincoln squadrons began to disband, commencing at Mildenhall on 23rd February 1950 when No.35 Squadron disbanded, followed a week later by Nos.115, 149 and 207 Squadrons. (All would subsequently reform in 1950/51 with Boeing B.29 Washingtons, followed in due course by Nos.15, 44, 57 and 90 Squadrons which also either reformed or re-equipped with the Washington).

In addition to the 22 squadrons mentioned, six other RAF squadrons would reform during the 1950s equipped, or partially so, with Lincolns for other duties and although the type finally departed Bomber Command in 1955/56, the last of the RAF's Lincolns continued to serve until 1963. It is intended to cover the period from 1950 to 1963 in a later volume.

An undated photograph of Lancaster B.1(FE[?]) TW909, No.35 Squadron. Seen at Khartoum, Sudan, unpainted and devoid of any unit markings with an Avro Tudor beyond. Reportedly this aircraft was only ever stored at MUs other than for a short period with No.35 Squadron from November 1947; it was sold for scrap in August 1948. However, according to one source at least, TW909 was the aircraft which conveyed the Commander-in-Chief, Bomber Command, Air Marshal Sir Norman Bottomley to the USA in conjunction with Operation *Goodwill*. Having departed Northolt, Middlesex, for the Azores on 20th July, they returned to the UK on 9th August 1946; needless to say a conflict of information exists here! via Tony O'Toole

A mixed unit formation comprising: camouflaged Lancaster B.1 NG340, 'KM-H' of No.44 Squadron; B.1(FE) TW893,'R' of (most likely) No.138 Squadron but possibly No.115 Squadron; B.1(FE) TW891, 'NF-K' of No.138 Squadron. Although undated, by September 1947 NG340 had become ground instructional machine 6421M; equally relevant is the fact that by June 1947, No.44 Squadron's Lancasters had virtually been replaced by Lincolns. Moreover, No.138 Squadron changed its code from 'AC' to 'NF' in December 1946, implying therefore that this is a 1947 photograph and that non-FE standard Lancasters were still operational, albeit in NG340's case apparently unarmed and with the dorsal turret removed. TW893 later served with No.230 Operational Conversion Unit (OCU) and was sold on 25th November 1949 and delivered to the Royal Egyptian Air Force in August 1950, numbered 1804. TW891 went on to serve with No.49 Squadron before being sold for scrap in mid-1950. Newark Air Museum

Above: Lancaster B.1 LM274, 'QR-F' of No.61 Squadron. Delivered in August 1944 and seen between mid-1945 and April 1946, when it was SOC, LM274 was an old warhorse that had survived 69 missions during WWII. Post-war it was already on borrowed time as, having accumulated in excess of 690 flying hours, the aircraft comfortably exceeded Bomber Command's desired peacetime maximum of 150 hours 'on the clock'. Number 61 Squadron continued to use Lancasters until mid-1946; by then Lincolns were on strength and they were retained until mid-1954. *Newark Air Museum*

Below: Lancaster B.7(FE) NX692, EP-? of No.104 Squadron, seen in Egypt at either Abu Sueir or Shallufa in 1946/47, in company with several Spitfire Mk.9s. Three engines have been removed from NX692, as has the Martin dorsal turret, its location having been plated over. Many crews considered the dorsal turret's location in the B.7 to be a particular hindrance. NX692 was only operated by No.104 Squadron and received the individual code 'D', 'R' and 'Y' at various times until it was SOC in November 1947. Number 104 Squadron, as with No.40, 70 (ex-178) and 37(ex-214) Squadrons were all disbanded on 1st April 1947, while No.205 (Heavy Bomber) Group, to which they all belonged, had been disbanded the previous day. *Tony Buttler Collection*

Above: Lancaster B.1(FE) SW299, 'OJ-U ' of No.149 Squadron, with black-painted rudders. Built in June 1945, SW299 went into storage prior to being issued to this Squadron, the only unit to operate it. SW299 was scrapped in December 1949, shortly after the Squadron had begun re-equipping with Lincolns, which was short-lived as No.149 Squadron disbanded on 1st March 1950. (It reformed again in August and in November 1950 became the first Bomber Command squadron to receive the B.29 Washington.) Brandon White

Below: Lancaster B.1(FE) PA383, 'KO-H' No.115 Squadron, Mildenhall, Suffolk, 1949. Having been completed as a B.1, PA383 was subsequently modified to FE standard and allocated to No.115 Squadron with which it received the individual codes 'D','K' and 'H' at various times. Only ever operated by this unit, PA383 made a belly landing on three engines, the port-outer having been feathered, at Mildenhall on 26th May 1949, the end result being seen here. Some sources state that the incident occurred on 26th April, but, whichever, PA383 didn't fly again. Having received B.1(FE)s in 1946, No.115 Squadron retained its last into January 1950, conversion onto Lincolns having commenced in September 1949. The Squadron was disbanded on 1st March 1950, reforming with Washingtons three months later. via Roger Lindsay

Below: Lancaster B.7(FE) NX780, 'KC-?' No.617 Squadron, in near pristine condition. This Squadron received its first B.7(FE) in mid-1945, with NX780 joining the unit in December of that year. Having returned from India (as previously related), No.617 Squadron retained Lancasters until the latter part of 1946, although their replacement by Lincolns had commenced during September that year. NX780 was reallocated to the RAF Technical College at Henlow, Bedfordshire and eventually sold for scrap in December 1954. Newark Air Museum

Above: Lancaster B.7(FE) NX791, 'KC-E' ex-No.617 Squadron, stored in less than pristine condition at Aston Down, Gloucestershire. Aston Down was the site of No.20 MU, which became important in the Post-war years for the storage, processing and dismantling of war surplus aircraft before closing on 30th September 1960. With its rudders removed and in poor external condition, NX791 appears fit only for scrapping, however, it was refurbished and later issued to the RAF Flying College (RAFFC) at Manby, Lincolnshire in October 1949. It was eventually SOC in November 1953. Newark Air Museum

Below: Lancaster IV (later Lincoln) prototype PW925, seen at Ringway (today's Manchester Airport) between 9th June 1944, the day of its maiden flight and 13th June, the day that it was delivered to Boscombe Down. PW925 was followed by two further prototypes: PW929 and PW932 which first flew in November 1944 and November 1945 respectively, although sources conflict re the date of the latter's first flight. In this image PW925 lacks defensive armament, is fitted with three-bladed propellers, has the symbol 'P' (prototype) applied to the fuselage and has had an astrodome fitted at the rear of the cockpit (applied prior to its maiden flight). The white lines on the wings appear to be peeling off in some areas and might therefore have been some form of temporarily applied tape. Ahead of PW925 are four Avro Ansons and three Westland Lysanders. Newark Air Museum

Top: Lincoln B.2 RF532, 'LS-D' No.15 Squadron, September 1948. This aircraft was operated by Nos.15 and 44 Squadrons before returning to No.15 Squadron once more, and was ultimately sold for scrap in May 1955, several years after the Squadron had ceased using Lincolns in October 1950. Number 15 Squadron was the unit chosen to fulfil a post-war requirement for at least one squadron to be equipped (or partially equipped) with Lincolns capable of carrying a 12,000lb 'Tallboy' deep penetration bomb internally. In order to enclose the bomb, the Lincolns chosen required enlarged bomb doors which thus provided them with a more bulbous profile than the norm.
Newark Air Museum

Above: A familiar image of factory-fresh Lincoln B.2 RF355. Built within a batch of 200 Lincolns (two B.1s and 198 B.2s) and delivered between March 1945 and May 1947, this aircraft served with Nos.12, 214 (twice), 49, and 7 Squadrons prior to being sold for scrap in April 1956. The blister below RF355's fuselage is a radome which contained an H2S radar scanner, the version seen here being the 'small' variant, more properly termed Mk IIIG. Much larger was the radome that later accommodated the H2S Mk IVA, and images exist which show that RF355 later received this larger variant. From February 1947, H2S-equipped Lincolns were designated accordingly as B.II/IIIG or B.II/IVA (later B.2/3G and B.2/4A respectively). No.9 Squadron apparently became the first operational unit to receive Mk 4A-equipped Lincolns in 1949; two years later than intended! Author's collection

Above and opposite page: Lincoln B.2 RF445, 'KM-G' No.44 Squadron, Rhodesia, June 1948. Number 44 (Rhodesia) Squadron, having conducted service trials with the Lincoln in 1945, finally bade farewell to the Lancaster and became fully equipped with Lincolns during May/June 1947. In 1948 the Squadron was despatched to pay a long-awaited visit to the country whose name the unit bore, and this and the following images of No.44's Lincolns herald from that visit. Each of these images were originally developed at studios in either Salisbury or Bulawayo in a country which is today called Zimbabwe. The Squadron retained Lincolns until January 1951 and re-equipped with Washingtons shortly thereafter. RF445 served until scrapped in August 1957, having operated in turn with the Airborne Forces Experimental Establishment, Nos.50 and 44 Squadrons, Central Gunnery School (CGS) and the Coastal Command Gunnery School (CCGS); the latter formed on 1st January 1955 from elements of the CGS which had disbanded the previous day. Author's collection and Newark Air Museum

Right: Number 44 Squadron's Badge appeared on both sides of their aircraft's forward fuselage and consists of an African elephant on a mount and is not be confused with that of No.27 Squadron's Badge featuring an Indian elephant, (small ears). The motto of No.44 Squadron translated reads 'The King's thunderbolts are righteous'. The elephant symbolises a heavy attack.
Newark Air Museum

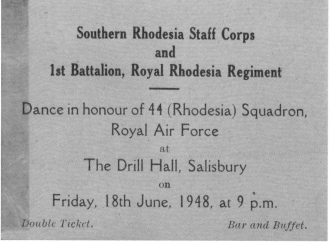

Southern Rhodesia Staff Corps
and
1st Battalion, Royal Rhodesia Regiment

———

Dance in honour of 44 (Rhodesia) Squadron,
Royal Air Force
at
The Drill Hall, Salisbury
on
Friday, 18th June, 1948, at 9 p.m.

Double Ticket.   Bar and Buffet.

A poor quality air-to-air image of an unidentified Lincoln in flight, although its unit code would appear to be 'KM-K'. The 'bouncing bomb' is in fact the H2S Mk3G radome.
Author's collection

Above: Lincoln B.2 RF405, 'VN-?' No.50 Squadron, Waddington 1948. Number 50 Squadron received Lincolns from July 1946 and retained them until the unit disbanded on 31st January 1951. RF405 was operated in turn by Nos.57, 50, 57 and 50 Squadrons following which it was transferred to the RAFFC, where it obtained the unit code 'FGA-L'. The RAFFC was formed at Manby on 1st June 1949 and subsequently absorbed the Empire Flying School (EFS) and the Empire Air Armament School (EAAS). The College grouped its Lincolns and Handley Page Hastings into one integral unit during the 1950s known as 'No.1 (Heavy) Squadron', although RF405 may not have been part of it as its flying days ceased in September 1954, when it became ground instructional airframe 7028M. The RAFFC was later renamed to become the College of Air Warfare (CAW) on 1st July 1962. Newark Air Museum

Opposite page: Lincoln B.2 RF385, 'DX-G' No.57 Sqn, seen in October 1945 while Lincoln Service trials were being conducted. This aircraft crashed between Queniborough and Barsby, Leicestershire, on 20th February 1946 during a storm. As the Lincoln commenced service, those originally destined for *Tiger Force* and the Pacific War were finished in the white and black colour scheme with a low demarcation line as applied to Lancaster FEs. Other Lincolns of the period were delivered in the then more familiar World War II

Temperate Land Scheme of Dark Earth, Dark Green and Night with a high demarcation line. RF385 displays the former scheme the upper surfaces of which, freshly applied, looked very smart and always remained so if, as the author was once informed by an ex-Lincoln navigator '…you never used the engines…'!
In August 1945, No.57 Squadron, then based at East Kirkby, Lincolnshire, had received a few Lincolns with which to conduct Service trials. Often stated to have been B.2s they are shown by two sources as having been B.1s RE285, RE286 and RE287; the latter two are certainly recorded as having been allocated to No.57 Squadron. However, other sources firmly state that the three Lincolns were B.2s RF385, RF386 and RF387! On 25th November 1945, the Squadron disbanded, although it was reformed a day later by the expedient of renumbering No.103 Squadron at Elsham Wolds, Lincolnshire. It appears however that the trials Lincolns were despatched to Scampton to form the Lincoln Service Trials Flight (LSTF) on that same day, 26th November 1945. The new No.57 Squadron (with 16 Lancasters), moved to Scampton in early December and became fully equipped with Lincolns by mid-1946, at which point it is presumed that the LSTF disbanded. The Squadron continued with Lincolns until April 1951 and subsequently converted to Washingtons.
Author's collection

Both photographs on this page and the first three images of the following page are all provided courtesy of Joe L'Estrange. Joe commenced his career as a turret gunner training first on Lancasters and later Lincolns in preparation for *Tiger Force*. Subsequently, Joe re-mustered as a pilot and opted to fly DH Hornets in the Far East before the RAF disposed of its last piston-engined fighters.
(See this publishers 'DH Hornet and Sea Hornet'.)

Above: **A flight of No.57 Squadron Lincolns, this being the Squadron in which Joe flew as a turret gunner.**

Below: **'DX-D' at Waddington.**

Left: Possibly RF407. If so this aircraft collided with Lincoln B.2 RE374, on exercise *Bulldog* during the night of 26/27th July 1949; all 14 crewmen were killed. By that time RF407 was operated by No.61 Squadron and RE374 with No.57 Squadron.

Below left and right: Joe L'Estrange in dorsal and tail turret respectively.

Below left: Lincoln B.2 RF447 'WP-P' Shallufa, Egypt 1948. Number 90 Squadron received Lincolns in April 1947, retaining its last Lancaster B.1(FE)s until the following September. On 1st September 1950, No.90 Squadron was disbanded and reformed a month later with Washingtons. This was the only flying unit to which RF447 is known to have been allocated; in February 1951 it received the maintenance serial 6830M. The names of the personnel are not known.
Author's collection

Bottom left: Unidentified Lincoln B.2, (but possibly RA669), 'OF-K', No.97 Squadron, 'somewhere in Cornwall in 1950'. This 'Box Brownie' image shows the aircraft to be fitted with the large, and in this instance, transparent radome which accommodated the H2S Mk 4A's scanner. Number 97 Squadron operated Lincolns from July 1946 until the last day of 1955, becoming 'Arrow' Squadron the following day and still equipped with Lincolns. Assuming this is RA669, it went on to serve with the Bomber Command Bombing School (BCBS) which formed in No.1 Group at Scampton on 15th October 1952.
Newark Air Museum

Above: **Lincoln B.2, RF472 'HW-B', No.100 Squadron, circa 1947.** RF472 was issued only to Nos.57 and No.100 Squadrons and is seen with its Hispano 20mm cannon installed in the Bristol Mk 17 dorsal turret. The Lincoln was one of only two types of aircraft in RAF service ever to be equipped with a duo of such powerful weapons mounted in a turret - the other being the Avro Shackleton. In service the dorsal turret was often removed as its location impeded progress in the fuselage and was thus considered by many to be a hindrance in peacetime, as too was its total weight of 1500lb; reportedly many of these redundant turrets were redirected to Shackletons. However, as regards the images shown in this volume at least, it would seem that it was the nose guns which were more commonly deleted rather than the dorsal turret! RF472 crashed on 15th March 1950 having overshot at RAF Hemswell, killing five of its six crew. *Newark Air Museum*

Opposite bottom: **Lincoln B.2 RF477, 'KC-?', No.617 Squadron.** This celebrated squadron had discarded its Lancaster B.7(FE)s by late 1946, having received Lincolns during the previous September; Lincolns were retained until January 1952 when they were replaced by English Electric Canberras. RF447 displays the Squadron Badge beneath the cockpit, which appropriately displays a wall breached by three lightning flashes and, issuing from the breach, a cascade of water; the Squadron motto translated reads 'After me, the flood'. Having served in turn with Nos.57, 100, 9, 617, 50, 617, 61, 100 and 61 Squadrons, RF447 went to the Ministry of Supply (MoS) during January 1955. Newark Air Museum

Above: **Lincoln B.2 RF513, 'KC-A', No.617 Squadron** with all guns fitted, a wing commander's pennant beneath the cockpit and with its bomb doors partially open. This was the first unit to which RF513 was issued

and therefore probably dates to early 1947; it was scrapped in October 1955. Other detachments apart, and following on from the success of No.35 Squadron's 1946 tour of the USA, No.617 Squadron undertook a goodwill tour of the USA and then Canada a year later. With 16 Lincolns, a few of which were brought in from other units in order to make up numbers, the squadron left the UK on 23rd July and returned to the UK on 9th September 1947. Author's collection

The image below was received just prior to going to press and is therefore included albeit outside of the established sequence.

Below: **Lancaster B.7(FE)s from No.617 Squadron on route to India in January 1946.** FAA Museum

2.

OTHER LANCASTERS, LINCOLNS AND UNITS: 1945–1950

From late-1945 onwards, with hundreds of otherwise redundant Lancaster airframes available, their utility for a host of training and other duties was not to be denied, which, to an extent applied to the Lincoln too. Although a comprehensive selection of each aircraft and 'other' units cannot be provided, it is hoped that those images which are included will provide a small indication of the differing duties and diversity with which they were employed.

In addition to those Lancasters seen in the photographs, the following – by no means exhaustive list, includes Lancasters that are known to have served with various other units from **circa** mid-1945 to late-1950. Those indicated serve merely as representative examples, they do not imply that they were the *only* ones to be allocated to a given unit; for instance, RE206 may have been one of several Lancasters in use with the Air-Sea Warfare Development Unit during its existence. (An equivalent listing for the Lincoln will be included in a later volume.)

Aries: *In Greek tradition meaning ram; named for the constellation of Aries and the flying ram with golden wool that rescued Phrixos and carried (navigated) him to the land of Colchis; the later destination of Jason and his Argonauts. (Following its epic flight, the ram was sacrificed to Zeus and its golden fleece hung in a tree to become the Argonaut's ultimate goal.)*

Above: **Lancaster B.1 PD328, 'Aries'. 'FGF' being the unit code and 'A' its individual code, Empire Air Navigation School (EANS), Blackbushe, Hampshire, 1946. The EANS formed on 28th October 1944, at Shawbury, Shropshire, from the Central Navigation School (CNS). Its role was to investigate the scientific advancement of navigational instruction and to research the development of new techniques designed to overcome problems associated with world-wide navigation. PD328's most challenging flight was its first assignment, which, although not perhaps the original intention, became in the event the first round-the-world flight of a British aircraft. PD328 (unnamed at this time), departed Shawbury for Prestwick, (Ayrshire), North America and the Pacific on 21st October 1944.**

Its task was to garner information on navigational aids and data, with a requirement to investigate and answer some long-perceived questions concerning the navigational problems and techniques associated with long-distance flight across the Pacific, (re *Tiger Force*), and to study US methods in combating the same problems. 'Aries' also visited Australia and New Zealand where its crew conducted lectures and established practical forms of liaison between the EANS and the air forces of those countries. The Lancaster and its crew of ten, (including a civilian navigation specialist) returned to the UK via the Mediterranean. The EANS continued as such until 31st July 1949, when it became the CNS once more. via Roger Lindsay

'Aries' PD328, Blackbushe, 1946, with its nose fuel tank being filled prior to commencing a flight to the Pacific. The tally of its other accomplishments are clearly chronicled on its nose accompanied by the School's Badge and Motif. Sometimes referred to as a 'Lancastrian' by virtue of the nose and tail fairings, it remained a Lancaster, receiving the modified nose and tail fairings seen in these images in 1945. 'Aries' was sold for scrap on 11th August 1948.
Newark Air Museum

Aeroplane & Armament Experimental Establishment - LL813, ME570, PA367, RF147, SW289

Air-Sea Warfare Development Unit - RE206

Aircraft Torpedo Development Unit - ME579

Blind Landing Experimental Unit - ME861

Bomber Command Film Unit - PD329, RF234

Bomber Command Instructors School - DV200, HK761

Bombing Development Unit - ME381

Bombing Trials Unit - TW923

Central Bomber Establishment - LL780, PB970, PB988

Central Flying School - NX696

Central Gunnery School - HK647

Central Navigation and Control School - NX773

Central Signals Establishment - ME535, PA421, PA444, PD381

Empire Air Armament School - LM451, NX632, PB873 (Thor)

Empire Air Navigation School - FM204, PD328, RT681, RT684

Empire Central Flying School - L7579, JA962

Empire Flying School JA962, NX687

Empire Test Pilots School - EE108

No.313 Ferry Training & Conversion Unit - FM172

No.1 Ferry Unit - LM734

No.12 Ferry Unit - FM106

No.16 Ferry Unit - PB915, RT672, SW320

Fleet Air Arm, No.780 Squadron, RN - NG232, PA224, RA513, RA528

No.1317 (Training) Flight - ND823

No.1323 (Automatic Gun Laying Turret Training) Flight - NE142

No.1347 (Air Sea Rescue) Flight - RF320

No.1348 (Air Sea Rescue) Flight - RF310

No.1577 (Airborne Experimental) Flight - JA903

Gee-H Training Flight - LM473

Joint Anti-Submarine School Flight - RF290

No.6 Lancaster Finishing School - R5855

No.230 Operational Conversion Unit - ME315, TW667

No.231 Operational Conversion Unit - R5855

No.236 Operational Conversion Unit - SW338

No.6 Operational Training Unit - PB179

Radio Warfare Establishment - ME383, ME535

RAF Flying College - NX687

Royal Aircraft Establishment - DS708, FM201, LM517, NX636, PP755, RF131, RT690

Special Installation Unit - NX618, RF147

Telecommunications Flying Unit - JB705, KB805, NX618

Transport Command Development Unit - PB532, RA510

Winter Research Establishment (a Canadian unit: RAF used facilities until 1949) - EE182, FM148 until 1949)

(Other than 'Aries', 'Thor', ED906, ED909 and PD137 which are treated separately, the following images are presented alphanumerically by serial number.)

'Aries' PD328, Blackbushe, 1946, during some last-minute servicing and protected by an armed guard.
Newark Air Museum

Below and opposite page: The EANS replaced 'Aries' PD328 with RE364 'Aries II', a specially adapted Lincoln B.2 in early 1947. As with its famous forebear, so too with RE364, which continued with the investigation of advanced navigational training and techniques, conducting numerous marathon flights in the process. The images shown here were taken during 1947 and include a chronology of flights undertaken which only appeared on the aircraft's starboard side. 'Aries II' was damaged beyond repair by fire at Shawbury on 26th January 1948.
Roger Lindsay

Above: Following the premature demise of 'Aries II' it was expedient to replace it, consequently Lincoln B.2, RE367 was selected for a conversion which was completed by the end of September 1948, and utilised some salvaged components from RE364. The image shown here is believed to have been taken in 1949, with RE367 undergoing deep maintenance and with the stylised name 'Aries' applied to its nose. Although commonly referred to as 'Aries III', the Roman number III is not included here. Roger Lindsay

Below: After a short period of service with the EANS, RE367 was transferred to the RAFFC. By the time that this photograph was taken, probably in 1950, the aircraft's livery was very different from the previous image, with the aircraft's name now depicted in plain capitals as was that of the College, reproduced in full, beneath 'ARIES'. The partially visible letters on the fuselage are '-AW', its full code was 'FG-AW', of which 'W' was the aircraft's individual identifying letter. Interestingly, photographs exist which show that they appeared grouped together as 'FGAW -' on the starboard fuselage. The codes were removed during 1951. RE367 continued in service until replaced by 'Aries IV', a Canberra, in September 1953 and was sold for scrap in January 1954. Roger Lindsay

Thor: The Norse god of thunder, the son of Odin, (and from whom Thursday is originated!)

Top: Lincoln B.2, RF523, 'Thor II' was delivered in July 1946 and later supplanted Lancaster B.I, PB873, 'Thor', both of which were operated by the Empire Air Armament School (EAAS) at Manby. 'Thor II' embarked on its first tour in late-1946, and flew to Canada and the USA, this image being obtained at Scott Field, Illinois in December of that year. In this, as with the other two images reproduced here, 'Thor' was fully armed and displays a mix of type 'D' roundels on its fuselage and wing upper surfaces with old style fin flashes; the serial on the fuselage is also further aft than was usual on most Lincolns. 'Thor II' went on to serve with the RAFFC after it absorbed the EAAS, and continued to serve with the College until 1953, although it was not sold for scrap until August 1957. Newark Air Museum

Above: Lincoln B.2, RF523, 'Thor II', at Changi, Singapore, 1948. Other than the anti-glare panel in front of the cockpit and the four spinner covers, RF523 was unpainted and does not display a unit code. The RAFFC retained Lincolns in diminishing quantities until 1960, although, as mentioned, RF523 had been disposed of by the College many years earlier. Author's collection

Below: 'Thor II' Seen here under public scrutiny, this Lincoln's principal duties were as much to do with armament and bombing systems training as it was with public relations and goodwill tours, for which it proved very popular. via Author

Top: Numbered amongst the veteran Lancasters that survived WWII was ED906, a survivor of Operation *Chastise*, the dam-busting raid conducted by No.617 Squadron in May 1943 and which had been flown on that occasion by Flight Lieutenant Maltby. Following service with No.617 Squadron and a period of storage, ED906 was allocated to Scampton's Station Flight, coded 'YF-A'. It is believed that this image was taken there during the second half of 1945 and, although modified to carry a 'Tallboy' bomb, the mounting arms for the 'Upkeep' mine (bouncing bomb) remain in-situ. By August 1946, this aircraft had been transferred to No.61 Squadron at Waddington, and was struck off charge on 29th July 1947 - and scrapped. Newark Air Museum

Above: A further survivor, for a while, was ED909 which had also served with the Scampton Station Flight - hence the code 'YF-B'; ED909 was also a survivor of the Dams raid, having been flown on that occasion by

Flight Lieutenant Martin. As with ED906, ED909 was allocated to No.61 Squadron and at some point thereafter became the ground instructional airframe 6242M, for duty with the Navigation Training Unit. 6242M/ED906 was struck off charge in July 1947 and scrapped at Scampton; probably the scene depicted here?
Newark Air Museum

Opposite page top: PD137 was a Lancaster B.I (Special), specifically adapted to convey a 'Grand Slam' deep penetration bomb, (later redefined as a medium capacity bomb), to its intended target. The bomb measured 25ft-5ins in length, had a maximum diameter of 46ins and contained 9,135lb of explosive for a total weight of 22,000lb. This made great demands on the carrier aircraft; it wasn't merely a question of dragging such a bomb a few feet into the air - to be effective high altitude was required, the higher the better in order to create the

deepest possible penetration of the target, or, in the case of a near miss, an 'earthquake'. One of 32 B.1(Specials) built and delivered between January and March 1945, PD137 was never issued to a squadron, but went instead to the Bomb Ballistics Unit (BBU) which moved from Woodbridge, Suffolk, to nearby Martlesham Heath, on 12th April 1946. This photograph was taken at Farnborough in 1946 or 1947 and shows a Halifax in the background, while the Lancaster's 'third' (white) fin belongs to an Avro Tudor. Subsequently, following a period of storage, PD137 was transferred to the RAE at Farnborough, where it arrived on 25th April 1950 to undertake heavyweight parachute trials. It was sold for scrap in April 1952. *Newark Air Museum*

Above: Lancaster B.3 ME545, 'V7-E', Radio Warfare Establishment (RWE), Watton, Norfolk, mid-1946. The RWE was formed at Swanton Morley, Norfolk, in July 1945 and relocated to Watton two months later. The RWE, in addition to other types, was equipped with a primary complement of 32 Halifax IIIs and Boeing B.17 Flying Fortress IIIs until April 1946, when all 32 were replaced with a like number of Lancasters. On 1st September 1946 the RWE became the Central Signals Establishment (CSE). ME545 had originally been allocated to No.218 Squadron as 'XH-L', with which it served operationally during the final months of WWII. The Squadron was disbanded in August 1945 and ME545 was sent to an MU prior to being allocated to the MWE, its dorsal turret having been removed and faired over. Retained by the CSE and for a time coded 'V7-Z', ME545 was removed from flying duties in June 1947 and received the maintenance serial 6295M. *Brandon White*

Above: Lancaster B.7(FE), NX739. This Lancaster in the event proved to be amongst the longest-lived of any to survive in British military or MoS service. It was first allocated to the English Electric Company in October 1945, following which it joined No.617 Squadron two months later and is believed to have participated in that unit's detachment to India. As related earlier, the Squadron re-equipped with Lincolns from September 1946, and NX739 was despatched to No.20 MU, presumably wearing the FE colour scheme. Because of its longevity, several images of this aircraft exist, many of which were taken in 1956/57, at Blackbushe, where NX739 was then based; however, this image pre-dates them, although to which side of this volume's 1950 watershed is uncertain. Of particular interest is the fact that this aircraft was repainted in a pattern better associated with Lincolns: Medium Sea Grey upper surfaces and Anti-Searchlight Black lower surfaces with a high demarcation line; very few Lancasters carried this scheme. Other items of note include the bulged bomb bay doors and H2S radome, which was later removed. So, what of the intervening years? NX739 was maintained in excellent condition by 'Silver City Airways' and used as an official air-to-air and air-to-ground photography platform, retaining for a time all three turrets. In its day, it was sometimes referred to as the '...Lancaster in Fighter Command...' because, for administrative purposes, it fell nominally under that Command's purview. Author's collection

Below: Lancaster B.7(FE), NX739. This and the following image ought properly to appear in a subsequent volume, however, for the sake of comparison they appear here. Taken at Blackbushe in September 1956, NX739 was based there with 'Eagle Aviation', an associate of Harold Bamberg's 'Eagle Airways', and contracted to operate on behalf of the RAE at Farnborough to undertake MoS photographic work. Having arrived at Blackbushe on 13th October 1955, NX739 remained there until 16th January 1957, having appeared at the 1956 Farnborough Airshow in the interim. It was sold for scrap in July 1957. The 'bulge' under the fuselage where once the H2S radome had been located, is in fact the lower portion of the starboard tail fin. Newark Air Museum

Left: Clearly revealed in this familiar image are the enlarged bomb bay doors, as well as the Company's eagle motif which appeared in red on both sides of the cockpit. The dorsal turret had by this time been removed.
Newark Air Museum

Left and below left: **Lincoln B.2 RE304, Langar, Nottinghamshire, 29th March 1947.** It may look forlorn but RE304 was not a derelict, despite lacking engines and tail fins and subsequently went on to operate with the Central Navigation and Control School (CN&CS), the only unit with which it is known to have served. The CN&CS was formed at Shawbury in February 1950 by merging the CNS and School of Air Traffic Control (SoATC). By the time these images were taken, flying at Langar had practically ceased at the end of 1946, and the airfield was closed. Despite this, Avro maintained a company presence there, particularly for the use of the workshop facilities that existed – which might offer some explanation as to RE304's presence there. RE304 was sold for scrap on 26th March 1957.
Both Newark Air Museum

Above: Lincoln B.2 RF350, 'SN-L' No.230 OCU, 1949. This OCU formed on 15th March 1947, at Lindholme, Yorkshire, out of No.1653 HCU; its full title was No.230 (Heavy Bomber) Operational Conversion Unit. Initially the unit was equipped with 16 Lancasters, plus a small complement of DH Mosquito night-fighters for fighter affiliation purposes. In February 1949, the OCU transferred to Scampton and re-equipped with Lincolns which were retained until disbanded in October 1952. In this image, RF350 clearly displays upon its nose No.230 OCU's motif which consists of a sword - hilt down, superimposed upon white and blue stripes; their motto being 'Temper the Sword'. Neatly framed by two spectators is the large H2S Mk4A radome, just entering service in 1949, (see Lincoln RF355 in Section 1 for details of H2S variations). RF350 went on to later serve with the BCBS and No.1321 Flight which reformed on 1st October 1957, at Hemswell, as an electronic countermeasures unit with seven examples of the Lincoln B.2/4A on strength; RF350 was sold for scrap in October 1958. Author's collection

Below and opposite page top: Lancaster B.1(FE) TW655, date and location unknown. As mentioned earlier, a post-war glut of Lancasters meant that many simply went straight into storage at various MUs and remained there without ever entering into active RAF service. TW655, seen in filthy external condition, was one of them - its total flying time amounted merely to the ferry time accrued whilst transferring from one

MU to another. Lacking background information, the assumption is that TW655 has been armed and suitably prepared to offer a war-like appearance for an open-day at either (first) No.46 or, (later) No.38 MU, the only two with which it was stored. Once more however, appearances deceive and, following a thorough overhaul, it went to France in 1952 as WU-17 of the Aeronavale. Damaged on landing at Port Lyautey, Morocco, it was SOC in October 1953.
Both Newark Air Museum

Below: Lancaster B.1(FE) TW669, date and location not known. This aircraft was converted to become a special photographic aircraft but it does not appear to have ever received a change in designation, e.g.

Lancaster PR.1 for instance. Equally its external appearance remains that of a standard B.1, with all three gun turrets retained; whether or not its external appearance ever altered remains unclear. Used by the Central Photographic Establishment Unit (CPE) at Benson, Oxfordshire, and the Air Photographic Development Unit (APDU) at the same location, it also became a 'Lancaster in Fighter Command' by virtue of its allocation to the Fighter Command Communication Squadron. In what order TW669 served these units isn't clear, but as the CPE and APDU both disbanded on 1st March 1950, it seems likely that this Lancaster served with those units first. TW669 was sold for scrap in February 1955. Newark Air Museum

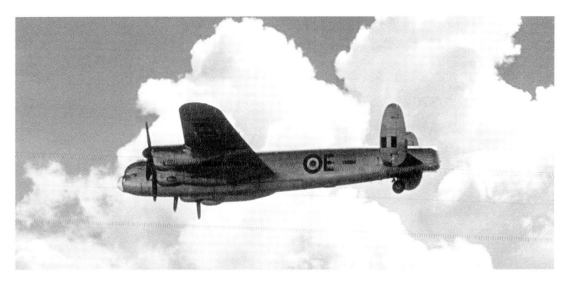

Top: Lancaster PR.1 TW904, 'E', No.82 Squadron, date unknown. Having served only with this unit TW904 was struck off charge in August 1950. Whilst Bomber Command had ostensibly ceased using Lancasters at squadron level by March 1950, some remained in service for a while longer, undertaking PR duties with adapted B.1s which had had their turrets faired over and a portion of the cockpit glazing painted or plated over. Operating under the auspices of Bomber Command, No.82 Squadron reformed on 1st October 1946, at Benson, from a nucleus of No.541 Squadron (PR Spitfires and Lancaster PR.1s) which had disbanded the previous day. The new unit was equipped with Spitfire PR.19s ('A' Flight), and Lancaster PR.1s ('B' Flight) and was employed in surveying Africa, covering the Gold Coast (now Ghana), Gambia, Nigeria and Sierra Leone, before relocating to Kenya to survey East Africa. Following its completion in late-October 1952, No.82 Squadron returned to Benson before moving to Wyton in the spring of 1953, where the PR.1s were gradually replaced by Canberra PR.3s. The unit's last Lancaster – and thus the last in Bomber Command proved to be PR.1, PA427, which was retired in December 1953 and later scrapped. Tony Buttler Collection

Undated images of unidentified Lancaster 'J9-H', from No.1668 HCU, at either Bottesford, Leicestershire or Cottesmore, Rutland at or near the war's end. No.1668 HCU relocated from the former to the latter base on 17th September 1945.
Both Newark Air Museum

Top: A poor quality but nevertheless evocative image of Lancaster B.7(FE)s stored at an undisclosed location. The airframe to the right appears to be NX703, if so, it was stored at Nos.32 and 38 MUs. Once again their external appearance seems poor, but in fact all, bar one - which is minus its rudders, have been shrouded to provide protection from the elements. NX703, if indeed that's what it is, was sold to France in 1952 to become WU-8 in the Aeronavale. It was scrapped in September 1958. Newark Air Museum

Above: On guard. Doubtless this image has a lot more to do with the handlers and their dogs rather than any aircraft, but it provides an interesting close-up of early Lincolns with three-bladed propellers and minus spinner caps. via Author

Right: An unidentified, thoroughly riddled Lancaster, at an unknown location on an unknown date.
Newark Air Museum

LANCASTERS

As a result of its size, airframe strength, multiple engines and consequent weight-lifting capability, the Lancaster proved to be a particularly useful vehicle with which to conduct trials of new engines, instruments, flight systems and weapons etc. By extension of course, the Lincoln also possessed the same attributes and proved to be just as useful in the field of aeronautical research as its predecessor. Comparatively large numbers of Lancasters and Lincolns served as test-beds, to use a generally accepted term, and the majority of their images will today be quite familiar to the reader. With this last point in mind, there follows a small selection of photographs which endeavour to portray a few of the lesser known research aircraft, or, failing that, then hopefully less well known images of the better known test-beds.

Above and opposite page: **Canadian Lancaster B.10, FM209.** Having been delivered originally to the RCAF, FM209 was transferred to A V Roe (Canada) Ltd, to be fitted with two Avro TR-5 Orenda turbojets in the outboard nacelles and was first flown in this condition on 13th July 1950, by which point the aircraft had been redesignated as a B.10 O. The Orenda was later fitted to several Canadair-built North American Sabre fighters and the Avro CF-100. FM209 was ultimately destroyed by fire on 24th July 1956.

The reader may question the inclusion of this aircraft here. However, after some deliberation, it was considered that as FM209 was one of only two Canadian Lancaster jet-engined test-beds of which this author is aware, these images are better placed here rather than within the RCAF section of the next volume. (Incidentally the other was FM205, which reportedly received two of just three Avro TR-4 Chinook turbojets to have been completed, although it never flew in that condition.) Newark Air Museum

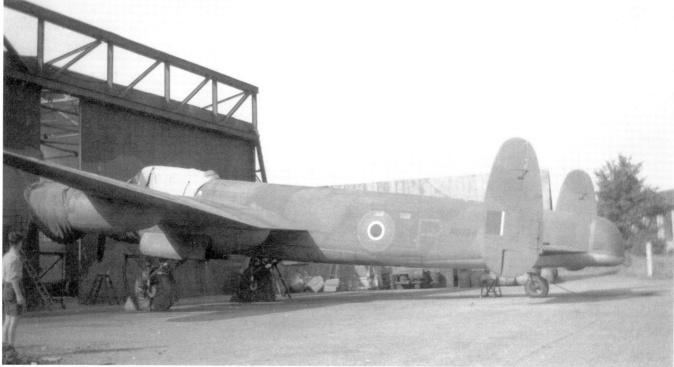

Top: Lancaster B.6 ND784, possibly at Bruntingthorpe, Leicestershire. Ordered as a B.3, this aircraft was one of just a handful converted to B.6 standard which included the installation of Merlin 85 engines as intended for the later Lincoln; the Merlin 85's distinctive engine cowls seen in this 1945 or 1946 image, are self-evident. Less evident is the Armstrong Siddeley 'ASX' (i.e. Armstrong Siddeley experimental) turbojet nestling in the Lancaster's open bomb bay; ND784's first flight with the ASX occurred on 28th September 1945. Following the ASX trials, ND784 received a radical nose conversion in order to receive the Armstrong Siddeley 'Mamba' turboprop engine. Newark Air Museum

Above: Lancaster B.6 ND784. An undated earlier image of ND784, bearing the letter 'P' (prototype) on its fuselage. There is no visible evidence of the alterations to the bomb bay which were required in order to accept the ASX engine, so it's possible that this is a late-WWII photograph of ND784 seen whilst awaiting conversion. Close study of this image shows that the aircraft's serial number has also been applied to the underside of the wing. ND784 was scrapped in 1951. Newark Air Museum

Top: An undated image of Lancaster B.1 NF910, on secondment to the de Havilland Aircraft Company. Having served operationally with No.467 Squadron from mid-1944, this Lancaster probably remained with the Squadron until it disbanded in September 1945. During August 1946, NF910 was allocated to de Havilland to conduct 4-bladed propeller trials; it ultimately came to grief on 9th June 1950, when it undershot and crash-landed at Moreton Valence, Gloucestershire, and was written off as a consequence. Newark Air Museum

Above: The concept of refuelling aircraft in flight was not new even at the start of WWII, but the perceived requirement to supply Tiger Force with Lancasters able to strike at Japan with a meaningful bomb load accelerated investigation into how it might best be achieved. The demise of Tiger Force removed some of the immediate imperatives of in-flight refuelling, but the advent of jet-powered fighters into the RAF, particularly the Meteor, imposed others by virtue of their insatiable appetite for fuel, ergo – a very limited endurance. Following pioneering work conducted by Flight Refuelling Ltd (FRL), the hose and drogue method of refuelling became established and remains standard with the RAF to this day. This image may have been taken at Staverton, Gloucestershire, where PB972 arrived in March 1945. Presumably it was delivered as a standard Lancaster and was later extensively modified to explore the various methods of in-flight refuelling then being trialled? Courtesy of Simon Watson

Top: Ought this somewhat familiar image have been included or not? If nothing else it illustrates the very first occasion on which the hose and drogue method of refuelling was used to transfer fuel, in flight, between Meteor F.3 EE397 and Lancaster G-33-2 (ex-PB972). The date was 24th April 1949, and the Meteor pilot made three link-ups without any apparent problems. Four months later the same pilot achieved a record endurance for a Meteor by remaining airborne for a little over 12 hours – proof that this method of in-flight refuelling was viable. The Lancaster's markings 'G-33-2' was a 'B condition' identification rather than a registration and FRL was allocated 'G-33' on 1st January 1948. G-33-1 was allocated to another Lancaster (ex-ND648), and it appears that it plus G-33-2 were the only two such identities to have been taken up by the company. via Author

Above: Lancaster B.3 RE131. Having served operationally with Nos.44, 75 and 207 Squadrons, RE131 went into storage on 10th November 1945 until 18th July 1947. At some point thereafter it was allocated to the Bristol Aircraft Company at Filton, Gloucestershire, and was fitted with a scale version of the Brabazon airliner's control system. RE131 was retained on this project until 1949, after which there is little information beyond the fact that it survived until April 1953. Other images exist of this aircraft at Filton with the dorsal and rear turrets still in-situ in 1947/48, however in this image, the former has been removed and faired over and the latter replaced. The starboard tail fin has obscured the letter 'P', although its encompassing circle is partially visible to the rear of the roundel, and the H2S radome remains in place. The distant aircraft is an Avro Anson. Simon Watson

Top: Lancaster B.3 SW342. This aircraft was first delivered to FRL at Staverton in September 1945, was later transferred to Air Service Training (AST) at Hamble, near Southampton in March 1947 and then despatched to Armstrong Siddeley (AS) at Bitteswell, Leicestershire, in January 1949. There it was adapted to carry an AS Mamba turboprop in its nose and later the same engine was equipped with a cropped propeller with an icing rig fitted ahead of it. Meanwhile, at SW342's other end, an AS Adder turbojet was installed in May 1952, to which an afterburner was later added. Finally an AS Viper was fitted and tested. SW342 was scrapped in June 1956. In this image the icing rig in front of the nose is apparent, as is an air intake and either an Adder or Viper turbojet in the Lancaster's tail. Newark Air Museum

Above: Amongst the most photographed and best documented of all Lancaster test-beds, TW911 was built by Armstrong Whitworth, completed in March 1946 and retained by that company for trials. Fitted with two AS Python contra-rotating turboprops in the outer nacelles, the Python ultimately proved successful enough to become the power plant for the Royal Navy's Westland Wyvern, S.4 strike aircraft. Photographed on 17th February 1950, TW911 was struck off charge in January 1953. Newark Air Museum

LINCOLNS

Opposite page top: Lincoln B.2, RA657 was loaned to FRL in September 1949 to help further develop the hose and drogue method of in-flight refuelling. Having been suitably modified as an aerial tanker, RA657 was employed a year later in the first successful east-west non-stop crossing of the Atlantic by jet aircraft of the USAF. The crossing was made on 22nd September 1950, with two USAF Republic F-84 Thunderjets employed in the attempt, one of which is seen in this photograph which was taken on that day. Following further refuelling trials, RA657 was later converted back to B.2 standard, returned to the RAF and allocated to No.199 Squadron at Hemswell. On 28th September 1956, this aircraft bounced whilst landing at Turnhouse, near Edinburgh, overshot the runway and went into a ditch – it was not repaired. via Author

Opposite page centre: Lincoln RE339. Built as a B.2 but used initially to trial Bristol Theseus turboprop engines, RE339 was operated for a time by the Lincoln Theseus Experimental Flight (LTEF), based at Lyneham, Wiltshire. The Flight came under the auspices of Transport Command; it was formed in April 1948 and allowed the Command to accrue experience with a type of engine that would later offer considerable improvements and benefits over their contemporary piston-engined transports. The LTEF disbanded in July 1950 and, with its involvement in Theseus trials complete, RE339 received two AS Python eight-bladed contra-rotating turboprops in lieu during 1950/51. They, as with the Theseus engines, were fitted in the two outboard positions with Merlins being retained inboard. The Pythons were powerful engines which allowed RE339 to achieve, for short periods of time, an altitude of over 40,000ft, with over 2,000 gallons of kerosene, 600 gallons of petrol and a 10,000lb bomb load on board. Ultimately, RE339 was used in conjunction with RF403 to conduct high altitude bomb ballistic trials in Australia, which included 12,000lb 'Tallboy' bombs. Although the latter had been used on many occasions towards the end of WWII, it had always been considered that with the altitudes then obtainable (20,000ft +), it didn't really allow for this bomb – let alone a 'Grand Slam' – to achieve its maximum penetrative capability. Presumably then, drops from 40,000ft did. RE339's location isn't supplied with this image, but it is fitted with Python engines and so could have been taken in Australia. Several references to this aircraft's serial give it as RE339/G i.e. Guard; however, in this image the letter G is not applied. RE339 was struck off charge on 3rd October 1956. Newark Air Museum

Opposite page bottom: Lincoln RE418. This Lincoln had much in common with RE339, and included participation in the development trials of the Bristol Theseus turboprop engine, which was fitted with a four-bladed propeller as seen in this image. RE418 also joined the LTEF and operated regularly between Lyneham and the Middle East. Although undated, RE418 bears Transport Commands Badge below the cockpit (applied to both sides of the fuselage), so most likely dates from mid-1948 or 1949. Having concluded its involvement with the Theseus engine, this Lincoln too was fitted with two AS Pythons in addition to its two Merlins. Newark Air Museum

Below: This photograph was taken at Fayid, Egypt, is dated 1st April 1950 and shows RE418 with its starboard Python turboprop undergoing maintenance and with both propellers removed. This aircraft too was despatched to Australia, although it was first sent to Bitteswell to be tested and was found to be capable of rising to an altitude of 35,000ft, at a maximum take-off weight of just under 70,000lbs. It was struck off charge in February 1953. Newark Air Museum

Above: Lincoln RF403. As with Lancaster TW911, Lincoln's RE339 and RE418, so to with RF403 which, as seen in this image, was also fitted with AS Python turboprop engines. At the time that this photograph was taken, RF403 was operating with a small fleet of Armstrong Siddeley test-beds based at Bitteswell. Later, following a period at Martlesham Heath, Suffolk, RF403 was despatched to Australia to conduct high altitude bomb ballistic trials above the Woomera weapons range. It was scrapped in New South Wales in 1958. Author's collection

Opposite page top: Ordered as a standard Lincoln B.2, SX972 was used instead in the development and trials of the Bristol Proteus turboprop engine as seen here. It first flew in this form in December 1950 and eventually completed 958 hours of flight testing, while the engine itself went on to power the Bristol Britannia airliner. SX972 was struck off charge in July 1953. Author's collection

4.

RAF MARITIME LANCASTERS, 1945 – 1950

As previously remarked upon, the end of WWII meant that the RAF's Liberators, both bomber and GR (general reconnaissance i.e. maritime) variants were to be returned to the USA under the terms of the Lend-Lease Act, scrapped, or purchased outright; the latter was not an option given Britain's financial position. The impending return of these aircraft would leave a capability gap which would have to be filled. The Lancaster's role as a bomber operating in the UK, the Middle and Far East has been earlier discussed; now its repertoire was to be expanded to include maritime reconnaissance and air-sea rescue (ASR) duties.

The genesis of an ASR capable Lancaster lay in the preparations for *Tiger Force*. For this, an adequate ASR capability had to be found given the vast tracts of Pacific Ocean over which bomber crews would fly, a task for which the existing twin-engined ASR Warwick was inadequate. Lancasters aiding other Lancasters was seen as a solution. With Rolls-Royce Merlin-powered FE standard Lancasters earmarked as *Tiger Force* bombers, Packard Merlin-powered Lancaster B.IIIs were selected for conversion to the ASR role, which included the ability to carry the same under slung Cunliffe-Owen 30ft 6in lifeboat as the Warwick which,

Above: Lancaster GR.3 RF311, 'CJ-G', No.203 Squadron c1950. Converted to an ASR.3 in 1946 there is no indication of service with any unit prior to being modified to GR.3 standard during 1949. Thereafter it was allocated to No.203 Squadron in September 1950, to No.15MU for storage before going to the School of Maritime Reconnaissance (SMR) as late as December 1955. It was sold for scrap on 25th May 1957. It is possible that this photograph was taken shortly after delivery to No.203 Squadron to judge by its very clean external condition; engine exhaust and oil stains having, as yet, barely affected the colour scheme of overall White with Medium Sea Grey upper surfaces. The unit code CJ was used on No.203 Squadron Lancasters from mid-1946 until 1951. The projection extending aft of the tail turret was fitted to a number of GR.3s (later MR.3s) as well as those Lancasters delivered to France and is believed to have contained a Strike camera and a flare chute; the flares being for night photography. Tony O'Toole collection

upon release, descended by parachute. Tested by Avro using a Lancaster B.I, the lifeboat was fitted beneath its (closed) bomb bay doors and secured to a specific member in the bomb bay originally designed to carry a 4,000lb bomb. A strut then descended from the bomb bay, through a set of small hinged doors cut into the bomb doors, and attached to the boat. Following these tests, the Cunliffe-Owen company was contracted to carry out conversions of 130 Lancaster B.IIIs to ASR.III standard – the first of which arrived at their Fastleigh Airport facility, near Southampton, in early 1945.

Several other alterations were to be applied including the fitting of two sets of directional antennas with which to pick-up distress messages and to triangulate its source if possible. H2S was retained, despite its known susceptibility to 'clutter' derived from various sea states. This was replaced in the later Lancaster GR.3/MR.3 variants (and to surviving ASR.3s upgraded to GR.3 level), by a much more suitable, purpose-designed, air-to-surface-vessel (ASV) radar set. To facilitate observation, a window was provided in the port-side fuselage ahead of the tail plane, while on the opposite side a window was cut into the fuselage door. The dorsal turret was removed.

Two units were due to receive the Lancaster ASR.III during 1945 – Nos.179 and 279 Squadrons – in readiness to form the Air Sea Rescue element of *Tiger*

Force. However the new variant was slow to enter service and by September 1945 only a single flight of No.279 Squadron, based at Beccles, Suffolk, had been fully equipped. With the ending of the war in the Pacific, conversion rates slowed considerably and, as the accompanying table shows, No.179 Squadron only received ASR.3s from February 1946, and some of those were transferred from a disbanding No.279 Squadron. The latter unit had also maintained a detachment at Pegu, Burma, and, with the disbanding of its parent body it assumed the title of No.1348 Flight.

With the demise of GR Liberators continuing through 1946 and into the following year, a somewhat more sophisticated replacement was needed than that provided by the Lancaster ASR.3 for the dedicated maritime reconnaissance role. The Lancaster GR.3 emerged to fulfil this role for which it received ASV radar plus other refinements, although it was still capable of carrying an airborne lifeboat should that necessity arise. As with the ASR.3, it too received the additional fuselage windows and the dorsal turret was removed. At a later date, the Lancaster GR.3 would be redesignated MR.3.

For ease of reference, the formation, disbanding or redesignation of Lancaster-equipped maritime reconnaissance squadrons is set out in the table overleaf.

Lancaster ASR.3 RF314, 'K7-LJ' No.236 OCU, 1947/48. Following its conversion this Lancaster served with Nos.179, 210 and 224 Squadrons before joining No.236 OCU, the identifying code of which was K7 during the period July 1947 to May 1951. Number 236 OCU was formed on 31st July 1947, at Kinloss, from No.6 Operational Training Unit (OTU). Its purpose was to train general reconnaissance aircrews for which it possessed an establishment of 20 GR.3s, plus an unspecified quantity of Lancaster ASR.3s and B.1s. The colour scheme of the ASR.3 depicted here was markedly different from RF311 and consisted of an Extra Dark Sea Grey and Dark Slate Grey disruptive camouflage scheme with Sky under-surfaces. RF314 ditched into the sea east of the Orkneys on 23rd July 1948, following the failure of three of its engines; the crew all survived.
FAA Museum

AIR-SEA RESCUE AND MARITIME RECONNAISSANCE LANCASTER SQUADRONS – 1945-1950.

Squadron	Period of service with Lancasters	Notes
No.18 Sqn	1/9/46 to 15/9/46	Equipped with the ASR.3, this unit reformed at Ein Shemer, Palestine, by renumbering No.621 Sqn. The new unit remained as such for 14 days, following which it was disbanded there, but remained in-situ, with its aircraft and crews being absorbed into No.38 Squadron.
No.37 Sqn	Sept 47 to 1953	Having disbanded as a bomber squadron at Fayid on 1/4/47, this unit reformed at Ein Shemer in September 1947, equipped with GR.3s for the maritime reconnaissance role and a responsibility to patrol the eastern Mediterranean. From April 1948, the Squadron began to redeploy from Palestine to Luqa, Malta, to beyond 1950.
No.38 Sqn	July 46 to 1954	Based at Luqa, No.38 Sqn operated Warwicks until approximately a dozen Lancaster ASR.3s were received, some reportedly from No.279 Sqn, but more probably from No.1348 Flight (see notes re No.279 Sqn). No.38 Sqn sent a detachment from Luqa to Ein Shemer on 15/9/46, to join the ex-No.18 Sqn aircraft and crews. By December the section in Palestine had been reinforced by the remainder of the Squadron, less a detachment retained at Malta. They returned to Luqa in April 1948 becoming (with No.37 Sqn), one of Malta's resident maritime reconnaissance units. During 1948, GR.3s supplemented the existing ASR.3s. The Squadron remained in Malta beyond 1950.
No.120 Sqn	Nov 46 to 1951	Reformed on 1/10/46 by renumbering No.160 Sqn at Leuchars. The new unit initially operated with a mixed complement of GR Liberators and Lancaster ASR.3s with a unit strength of just six aircraft. The Liberators were finally replaced in 1947, (possibly as late as June) by ASR.3s and GR.3s. In November 1947, this unit too was deployed to Palestine, following which it returned to Leuchars until it relocated to Kinloss, Moray in December 1950, in readiness to receive Shackleton MR.1s in early 1951.
No.160 Sqn	Sept 46 to Oct 46	Based at Leuchars since June 1946, and equipped with six GR Liberators, delivery of Lancasters commenced in August. However, on 30/9/46, No.160 Sqn was renumbered No.120 Sqn.
No.179 Sqn (and No.179X Sqn)	Feb 46 to Sept 46	Based at St Eval, Cornwall, this Warwick-equipped unit received a few Lancaster ASR.3s late of No.279 Squadron. The Lancaster element of the unit therefore became No.179X Sqn, while the Warwicks formed No.179Y Sqn. In May 1946, the Warwicks of No.179Y were disposed of and on 1st June that unit became No.210 Sqn, also based at St Eval. No.179X, reverting simply to No.179 Sqn, continued to operate Lancasters until disbanded on 30/9/46, at which point its aircraft and personnel were transferred to No.210 Sqn.
No.203 Sqn	Aug 46 to 1953	Having operated abroad since 1929, this unit returned to the UK in May 1946, equipped with GR Liberators. Based at Leuchars, the Squadron received Lancaster ASR.3s and GR.3s from August 1946 and had replaced the Liberators by October. In January 1947, the unit relocated to St Eval where it remained beyond 1950 flying maritime reconnaissance sorties primarily over the Western Approaches and participating in exercises.

No.210 Sqn	June 46 to 1952	Reformed by renumbering No.179Y Sqn on 1/6/46, the new unit was initially equipped with six ASR.3s and based at St Eval. Three months later the remainder of No.179 Sqn disbanded and transferred to join No.210 Sqn, which had also received their first GR.3s. Generally operating as per No.203 Sqn, No.210 Sqn also sent detachments to Ein Shemer to participate in anti-immigration patrols over the eastern Mediterranean from August 1947.
No.224 Sqn	Oct 46 to Nov 47	Based at St Eval since July 1945, No.224 Sqn's GR Liberators were replaced by Lancaster GR.3s during October 1946. These were operated for just over a year before the unit was disbanded in November 1947, at St Eval. Sources conflict as to whether or not ASR.3s were operated by the Squadron during its brief existence.
No.279 Sqn and No.1348 Flt	Sept 45 to Mar 46	Formed in November 1941, this Squadron was created specifically as an air-sea rescue unit and at war's end was equipped with Warwicks and Supermarine Sea Otters. On 3rd September 1945, No.279 Squadron moved to Beccles, Suffolk, and later that month both types were replaced by early production Lancaster ASR.3s. In December 1945, a detachment was sent to Pegu, Burma to provide ASR cover to the general area. Whilst there, the UK element of the Squadron was disbanded on 10th March 1946; consequently the detachment in Burma was absorbed by No.1348 (Air-Sea Rescue) Flight, which had relocated to Pegu two months previously. The Flight disbanded on 15th May 1946, its surviving Lancasters being sent to the Middle East to No.38 Sqn.
No.621 Sqn	Apr 46 to Sept 46	Already operating Warwicks in the ASR role from Aqir, Palestine, No.621 Sqn received Lancaster ASR.3s during late-April 1946. In June the unit transferred to Ein Shemer where, it would appear, the conversion process from Warwick to Lancaster was completed during August. However on 1/9/46 the unit was renumbered to become No.18 Sqn.

By 1st July 1948, operational maritime reconnaissance Lancaster squadrons had settled to the five units shown below. They were of course equipped with GR.3s and any remaining ASR.3s. Other than for temporary deployments and exercises, the unit's listed and their principal bases remained unchanged into 1950.

No.120 Sqn	Leuchars	No.18 Group, Coastal Command
No.203 Sqn	St Eval	No.19 Group, Coastal Command
No.210 Sqn	St Eval	No.19 Group, Coastal Command
No.37 Sqn	Luqa	Middle East Air Force
No.38 Sqn	Luqa	Middle East Air Force

Additionally, maritime Lancasters were operated by training units including: No.236 OCU, the Air-Sea Warfare Development Unit (ASWDU) and the Joint Anti-Submarine School (JASS). Details of these units may be found within captions accompanying the photographs.

KNOWN COASTAL COMMAND TWO-CHARACTER UNIT CODES

No.38 Sqn	RL	No.224 Sqn	XB	Those squadrons and units not included appear only
No.120 Sqn	BS	No.279 Sqn	RL	to have used single-letter identifiers.
No.160 Sqn	BS	No.1348 Flt	RL	
No.179 Sqn	OZ	No.236 OCU	K7	
No.203 Sqn	CJ	ASWDU	P9	
No.210 Sqn	OZ			

Top and centre: **Lancaster ASR.3, 'RF317'.** RF317 suffered a partial undercarriage collapse while taxiing at Colerne, Wiltshire, on 22nd February 1946 and was written-off. However, to the uninitiated - including the author, the two scenes depicted here seem to indicate an altogether more ferocious contact with the earth than a partial undercarriage collapse might otherwise suggest! Here the undercarriage is seen to be totally collapsed with both main wheels having been severed and both outboard motors torn from their mountings. So, with no serial number visible, is this in fact RF317? Although the dusty appearance of the ground and the presence of a Bristol Beaufighter in the distance might

suggest Burma and No.1348 Flight – which operated Beaufighters as well as ASR.3s, these scenes are *not* to be confused with the crash at Pegu of ASR.3, RF310, on 4th March 1946. Although RF310 was badly damaged, and subsequently written-off, examination of its crash-scene photographs show that both its starboard motors remained attached to the wing. *Brandon White collection*

Above: **Lancaster ASR.3.** This photograph might well hail from Burma which shows two unidentified ASR.3s at rest on a surface constructed from pierced-steel-planking and photographed over the starboard wing of a passing Liberator. *Brandon White collection*

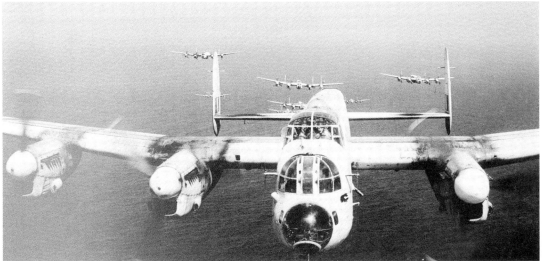

Left: Lancaster ASR.3 RF325, 'P9-J', Air-Sea Warfare Development Unit (ASWDU). Following conversion, RF325 served first with No.279 Squadron, then the ASWDU, following which it was converted to become a GR.3. Ultimately, this Lancaster came to prominence seven years later when, as an MR.3, it became the last Lancaster to officially fly in RAF service, a fact somewhat belied by its work-stained appearance in this 1949 photograph. RF325 made its last flight in October 1956 and was scrapped from July 1957, although large sections survived piled-up in a scrap yard into 1958 at least. The ASWDU was formed at Thorney Island, Sussex, on the first day of 1945, having formerly been the Coastal Command Development Unit. It moved to Ballykelly, Londonderry, in May 1948, to St Mawgan, Cornwall in May 1951 and returned to Ballykelly in 1958 where it disbanded in April 1970. P9 was the identifying code allocated to the ASWDU and was applied to the unit's Lancasters from early 1946 until late-1951 or early 1952. Ballykelly was also the home of the Joint Anti-Submarine School (JASS), which formed in November 1945 and operated several different types of aircraft, including Lancasters, for practising anti-submarine warfare.
Newark Air Museum

Centre and bottom: Lancaster GR.3s from the ASWDU in formation; location not known.
Both Brandon White collection

Above: Lancaster GR.3 SW283, 'OZ-U', No.210 Squadron. Converted first to an ASR.3 and later modified to GR.3 standard, this aircraft was first operated by No.279 Squadron followed by No.179 Squadron. When the latter unit began to disband from June 1946, it reformed as No.210 Squadron retaining the former Squadron's identity code OZ. These were retained until 1951, when Coastal Command commenced a change in the system of unit codes which were to be applied to its squadrons and other units. SW283 went on to serve with the SMR (which formed in 1951) at St Mawgan; it was sold for scrap in May 1957. Tony O'Toole collection

Below: Lancaster GR.3, SW319 'OZ-X', No.210 Squadron. Converted first to ASR.3 and later to GR.3 standard, SW319 served only with No.210 Squadron until SOC on 18th March 1950 when, whilst flying through cloud near Gibraltar, it was struck by lightning. Having landed safely, it was deemed not to be worth repairing. In late November 1949 the entire Squadron flew to Tengah, Singapore, for a two week tour, during which anti-submarine exercises were conducted. In this image SW319 has its guns mounted in the front turret and so, presumably, are the four .303s in the rear turret, although frequently none of the guns were carried. The Squadron's Motif, a Griffon, appears just below the cockpit and represents the Squadron's long association with Wales; its motto, translated from Welsh means 'Hovering in the heavens'. Newark Air Museum

Top: Lancaster ASR.3 SW368, No.203 Squadron, with a Cunliffe-Owen Airborne Lifeboat fitted below the fuselage. This aircraft later went on to serve with No.210 Squadron, followed by No.38 Squadron from May 1953 until, at a later date, it went to an MU for storage prior to being sold for scrap in May 1956.
Tony O'Toole collection

Above: A closer view of an under-slung Cunliffe-Owen Airborne Lifeboat. As can be seen it was a close-fitting arrangement in which the bomb bay doors remained closed; not apparent are the openings in the doors through which the boat was secured directly to the principal strength members of the bomb bay. If nothing else is identifiable in this image, the wheel chocks at least appear to belong to No.210 Squadron – assuming that it is their motif which appears upon them!
Author's collection

Above: Lancaster GR.3 SW368, 'CJ-L', still with No.203 Squadron. This photograph was taken at Negombo, Ceylon, during the 1950 air show which was held there and in which No.203 Squadron, or at least part of it, participated. *Dennis Sawkins via Brandon White*

Below: With RF312 leading, SW368 and two other GR.3s formate on their leader during the Negombo air show. RF312 was later badly damaged whilst landing at Coltishall, Norfolk, on 21st February 1952 and was not repaired. *Dennis Sawkins via Brandon White*

Top: Lancaster ASR.3 (later GR.3), TX264. This Lancaster formed part of the final batch of serials allocated to Lancaster production (as distinct from the final Lancasters built), TX263-TX273, which were delivered between 8th September and 31st October 1945, and all were then converted for use with Coastal Command. TX264 is seen in this image at Cunliffe-Owen's factory at Eastleigh, Hampshire, in June 1946. The aircraft, in pristine condition, looks as if it has just been rolled out, factory-fresh, on completion of its conversion complete with its own policeman. It was subsequently allocated to No.120 Squadron whose unit code was BS, and was applied to its Lancasters from December 1946 until 1951. TX264 remained with the Squadron until the night of 13th/14th March 1951, when it flew into high ground near Sail Mhor, Ross And Cromarty, killing all eight persons on board. The Lancaster had taken off from Kinloss for a six-hour reconnaissance of the Faeroes, but crashed into the mountain, Beinn Eighe, in the early hours of the 14th on its way back to Kinloss. Newark Air Museum

Above: A poor quality photograph illustrating three unidentified Lancasters, all are ASR.3s and all wear the unit code 'RL'. They are most likely therefore to belong to No.38 Squadron, although having obtained Lancasters from No.279 Squadron (and No.1348 Flight) their code RL was also adopted and used from July 1946 to 1951. The chances of it being a No.279 Squadron image are much reduced if the second aircraft 'RL-B' is SW293; if so it was never allocated to the latter unit. Having been converted to an ASR.3, SW293 was allocated in turn to Nos.37 and 38 Squadrons ('RL-B') prior to being converted to GR.3 standard. Thereafter it was operated by No.203 Squadron and the SMR before being sold for scrap in May 1957. Author's collection

5.

THE AVRO YORK

The Avro York, as with the Lincoln, was a direct development of the Lancaster. However, although the York was operated by the military, it was as a humble transport rather than a machine of war and therefore its story is rarely considered worthy of publication, an understandable yet unfortunate fact - hence its inclusion here. This section departs from the principles of those previous in that it offers a general overview of the York's military career from inception until its last days with the RAF in March 1957. For the most part the York's service with civilian operators remains outside of this publication's remit.

During World War II, Britain's aircraft industry was predictably and correctly dominated by the need to develop and produce combat aircraft. This in turn dictated that the country's (i.e. the military's) want of transport aircraft would have to be obtained by other means, principally by the adaptation of existing obsolete or obsolescent military aircraft, the use of impressed ex-civilian aircraft or those supplied by the US manufacturing industry.

For British manufacturers these measures would inevitably lead to a vacuum of development and design experience within the field of transport and passenger carrying aircraft. As a

Above: Avro York LV626, the first prototype. Photographed on 28th August 1942, eight days after its arrival with the A&AEE, and approximately seven weeks after its maiden flight on 5th July. LV626 had been received by the A&AEE to undertake preliminary performance and handling trials as well as ascertaining the aircraft's weight-lifting potential, to which end it was flown at an all-up-weight of 60,000lb using water as ballast. LV626 was in essence though an unfurnished shell, probably weighing less than 38,000lb empty, while production Yorks i.e. the pure freighter variants, possessed an empty weight of 39,500lb. (Passenger variants weighed approximately 42,050lb empty). The maximum all-up-weight for the York varies according to source, but appears to have been in the region of 65,000 to 68,000lbs, although it has been suggested that MW139 may once have been flown at almost 70,000lb! In this image, although hard to distinguish, it is possible to see the aircraft's original twin-fin configuration that was later amended to incorporate a third. The tail wheel was at this time partially recessed into the fuselage - also later amended, and the censor appears to have obscured the 'P' for prototype symbol from the rear of the fuselage. The photograph must have been taken on a very warm day, as the pilot is in shirtsleeves with his window wide open; either that or wind noise was preferable to the noise levels generated in the interior of almost any York – which was said to be excessive! via Author

Above: Avro York LV626. Although undated this image must post-date 17th March 1944, which was the date of this aircraft's first flight fitted with 1,650hp Bristol Hercules radial engines to become the solitary York II. Previously it had flown with the 1,280hp Merlins seen in the previous image. Additionally, LV626 had by this time received a third fin and a different tail wheel arrangement. By late-March 1945, LV626 had been sent to No.46 MU for conversion to a ground instructional airframe and by the following August resided at St Mawgan, serialled 5554M. Newark Air Museum

Below: The third prototype (and second to fly), Avro York LV633 was easily identified by its angular windows. This image shows the unique 'Ascalon' as it appeared post-war, following its earlier career as one of the principle modes of wartime transport used by Prime Minister Churchill until superseded by Douglas C-54 Skymaster EW999,

(ex-USAAF 43-17126) in late 1944. Although undated, this photograph was taken at Avro's facility at Langar and it is known that LV633 spent almost two years there, between May 1947 and March 1949, undergoing both repairs and overhaul; its pristine condition, overall Aluminium finish and post-war national markings suggest that this image was taken shortly after that work had been completed. Subsequently, following a period in storage, LV633 was allocated to the Far East Air Force (FEAF) Communication Squadron's VIP Flight at Changi, Singapore. It arrived there in October 1951 and remained until early April 1954, when it was flown back to the UK and struck off charge on the 10th and thereafter scrapped. It was replaced by 'Ascalon II', MW295, which in the event proved to be the last York in RAF service when retired in March 1957 to be replaced by VIP Handley Page Hastings C.4s. (See this publishers title *Hastings: Handley Page's Post War Transport Aircraft*). Newark Air Museum

Above: VIP York MW100, the first of the production Yorks to be completed and possibly photographed during acceptance flights in October 1943, the month that it was accepted into the RAF at Northolt as well as No.511 Squadron which maintained a detachment there. Later, in September 1944, MW100 was transferred to the Metropolitan Communications Squadron (MCS) which, though based at Hendon, Middlesex, maintained three VIP Yorks at Northolt. In this image MW100 is very obviously camouflaged, but less obviously the engine exhausts are shrouded. via Author

Above: VIP York MW100. At war's end, this York was being operated by No.246 Squadron which also maintained a detachment of Yorks at Northolt. Thereafter it served with various units as well as undergoing periods of repair and modification. As seen in this undated image, the opportunity had previously been taken at some point to remove both camouflage and exhaust shrouds; the individual exhaust stubs now being visible. MW100 is seen having delivered General Sir Alan Cunningham, the High Commissioner of Palestine and Transjordan, to Lydda, Palestine. Cunningham held this position from November 1945 until mid-1948, after which Palestine ceased to exist. Regarded perhaps as a poisoned chalice, the armed guard and armoured car in the foreground were not there for ceremonial reasons alone! The caption on the rear of the photograph suggests that this was his first visit to Palestine as High Commissioner and so would date this photograph to late-1945 or early 1946. MW100 was despatched to an MU in November 1951 and offered for sale during the following October. It was sold to Surrey Flying Services in May 1953 and allocated the civil identity G-ANAA, which was not taken up and the aircraft was broken-up for spares in 1955.
Newark Air Museum

result, US aircraft manufacturers were well placed to dominate particularly in a post-war era that would one day surely arrive.

Such concerns were recognised by individuals within Britain's aircraft manufacturing industry quite early on in WWII, amongst whom was Roy Chadwick at Avro. Additionally, following America's entry into the war, Britain's Air Ministry evinced concern as to whether or not even the USA would be able to supply all of their own as well as British transport aircraft requirements in the years ahead. Consequently, in January 1942, the Air Ministry gave notice that it wished to further examine a proposal for a transport aircraft, designed by Chadwick, which they had originally considered in October 1941; one which made full use of a Lancaster's components but which substituted the latter's fuselage for one which was essentially square in section and capacious.

The Air Ministry's response proved encouraging and, without delaying for anything as trivial as formal approval from the Ministry, Chadwick had plans drawn up for the Avro Type 685 transport. On 24th March 1942, the Ministry of Aircraft Production (MAP) authorised the construction of two prototypes, followed by two more in mid-April, whilst their collective contract followed in early May 1942. The four proto-

types were serialed: LV626, LV629, LV633 and LV639. Concerns regarding the availability of Merlin engines caused MAP to require that two of these four aircraft should be fitted with Hercules engines, although in the event only one, LV626, was so equipped – receiving them at a later date in lieu of the Merlin engines originally fitted.

The first flight of a Type 685 occurred when LV626 took to the air on 5th July 1942. All went well although it was revealed that the type would benefit by the receipt of additional fin area to increase lateral stability. This was later acted upon and a third, centrally placed fin was added, a refinement that was incorporated on the production line from the third prototype onwards. At this time LV626 was, more-or-less, an empty shell without internal fittings and was not then representative of later production aircraft, it having previously been decided to use it principally for flight testing purposes and as a test-bed for the Hercules power plant – with which it was first flown on 17th March 1944. The Hercules flight trials progressed well and with little fuss, there being only a negligible difference in performance and handling with either type of engine, otherwise, perhaps the most noteworthy change was one of nomenclature – as radial-engined LV262 became the solitary mark II.

Avro York 'MW100'. For the record, MW100 is today represented at the National Cold War Exhibition, (part of the Royal Air Force Museum located at Cosford Airfield, Shropshire,) by York C.1, ex-'LV633' ex-G-AGNV, ex-TS798, one of 60 ordered in November 1944 to meet a combined RAF/BOAC requirement. The RAF portion was subsequently cancelled leaving 25 passenger/freighter variants for BOAC in the serial range TS789 to TS813 inclusive, which, although initially applied in many instances, were quickly replaced by civil registrations before entering service. (Also, see colour images of 'LV633'- 'Ascalon' on page 97.)
Newark Air Museum

York G-AGNV, ex-TS798 (later to become 'LV633' and 'MW100') seen in revenue earning service with Skyways of London, on 20th July 1958, at Luton Airport, Bedfordshire.

Although no official specification had been written by the time of LV626's first flight, it was envisaged that the aircraft should be capable of conducting a number of transport orientated roles. Eventually, Operational Requirement No.113 was released in mid-July 1942 which specified that the type should be capable of the following duties: Transportation of 24 passengers – or a lesser number of stretchers if operating in an ambulance role; long-distance heavy freight operations; transportation of 30 troops or paratroops with respective equipment, weapons and supply containers. It was further intended that it should be able to act as a glider-tug when required – and that the aircraft should be capable of being adapted from one role to another within a 24 hour period. (In practice this last requirement proved to be a complex, sometimes difficult undertaking not easily accomplished within 24 hours!)

On 18th August, a production order was placed for 200 Yorks, as the aircraft had by now been named. It was expected to achieve a range of 2,950 miles at 20,000ft with an 8,000lb load and was to be able to accept either Merlin or Hercules engines as necessitated by the demand for one or the other. (As stated, only LV626 ever flew with Hercules engines, all other Yorks were Merlin-powered, becoming the Mark I, later C.I, then C.1.)

Whatever the intended plans for the third prototype were, they were altered completely when Avro was instructed in September 1942 to convert LV633 for use by HM King George VI or the Prime Minister, Winston Churchill. Its interior was to be transformed to VVIP status with accommodation for sleeping berths, a conference and a state room plus rectangular windows. Avro was instructed to deliver it by January

1943, but delay was caused by order, counter-order and confusion; however, it was completed during March 1943 and, following trials and testing, it commenced from 25th May a career as 'Ascalon', named after the lance (or sword – dependant on source) used by St. George to slay the dragon. Following on from the VVIP LV633, the decision was taken in January 1943, that the first three production Yorks (MW100, MW101 and MW102) would also be fitted with a high-standard interior, albeit to the lesser VIP standard accommodating up to ten seats forward plus sleeping bunks aft. Additionally, a quantity of Yorks were completed as first class passenger aircraft for the RAF accommodating 24 passenger seats and a somewhat lesser degree of comfort than that found in the VIP versions.

Because of the Lancaster's priority, York production was slow with only MW100, MW101 and MW102 being delivered to the RAF in 1943, during October, November and December respectively. The first non-VIP York to reach the RAF was first class passenger-equipped MW104 in February 1944, its immediate predecessor MW103 having been allocated to the British Overseas Aircraft Corporation (BOAC) in January 1944, shortly after its completion. Four further Yorks were also delivered from RAF contracts to BOAC, all of which were completed as first class passenger aircraft. The five were:

MW103: transferred on 31st January 1944; re-registered as G-AGJA.

MW108: transferred on 19th April 1944; re-registered as G-AGJB.

MW113: transferred on 30th May 1944; re-registered as G-AGJC.

MW121: transferred in late July 1944; re-registered as G-AGJD.

MW129: transferred in September 1944; re-registered as G-AGJE.

(In addition, during November 1946, MW320 was also diverted from RAF contract to Skyways Ltd and registered G-AIUP.)

MW104's delivery was followed by that of MW105 in the same month, the latter being the first of the dedicated freight-carrying Yorks as opposed to those completed as VVIP, VIP or first class passenger aircraft. Later, in April 1945, a further variation made its debut as a combined passenger/freighter equipped with 24 passenger seats which, when required, could be removed allowing such Yorks to be operated in a single-role capacity. The first passenger/freighter York to be completed was MW169, which was later to be allocated to General de Gaulle as his personal transport aircraft. MW105's completion incidentally, predated that of prototypes LV629 and LV639, neither of which were completed until March 1944, possibly later! Both were used for various trials, although it was with the latter that the suitability of the York as a glider-tug

was found wanting, as the aircraft's fuselage produced severe turbulence in its wake which proved dangerous for the glider beyond. It proved dangerous for paratroopers too.

In April 1943, as the first production order of 200 Yorks seemed likely to gather pace, a further wartime order for 100 Yorks was placed with Avro, while a further order for 50 was placed that year with Victory Aircraft in Canada. Ultimately, however, the new order placed with Avro was reduced first to 36 aircraft in February 1946, then, four months later, was further reduced to just eight that later emerged as PE101-PE108. The Canadian order was reduced to just one example during 1944, which, following completion towards the end of that year became FM400, the solitary York C.III. Briefly operated by the RAF, FM400 was sold to Skyways Ltd in 1948, following almost two years in storage. As for the original order, it would seem that perhaps 42 Yorks were completed during 1944, approximately 55 in 1945, with the remainder being completed in 1946 and 1947. PE101-PE108 were delivered during 1947 and 1948, with PE107 and PE108 being the last two Yorks to be received by the RAF, both of which flew for the first time on 12th

Left and below left:
Two images of VIP York MW101, neither are dated and offer little information as regards location or duty. Quite obviously they were taken at different times as indicated by the application of different styles of national markings, the image with the armed guard being the earlier of the two which also displays (albeit poorly) Transport Command's Motif below the cockpit. Their motto translated read 'I strike by carrying'. The later image is simply captioned 'FEAF'; in fact MW101 was allocated to the FEAF and arrived at Singapore in January 1951 to join the FEAF Communication Squadron. However, it was damaged and returned to the UK eight months later and, having languished at an MU, was sold for scrap in June 1955.
Tony Buttler Collection and Newark Air Museum

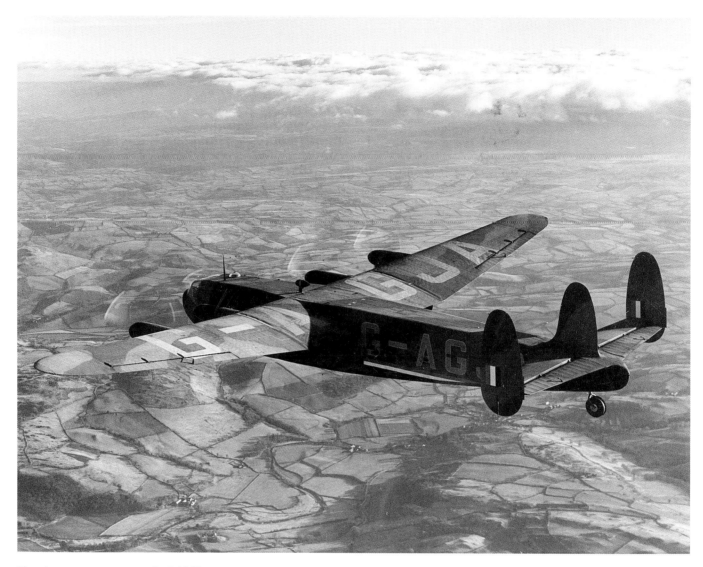

First class passenger-equipped York C.1, G-AGJA. This aircraft had been ordered for the RAF as MW103, hence its inclusion here, although it seems likely that the military serial, though allocated, might never have been applied. Diverted from an RAF contract shortly after completion, MW103 was officially transferred to BOAC at the end of January 1944 and subsequently named 'Mildenhall'. via Author

April 1948; they were sold as scrap in 1955 and 1953 respectively following several years in storage.

The period 1948 into 1949 would prove to be the period for which the York (other than 'Ascalon') came to prominence – in so far as any transport aircraft could do. This was the occasion of the Berlin Airlift, or, Operation *Plainfare*, prior to which, the RAF's Yorks had been mainly employed in providing a regular long-distance aerial service linking the UK with empire, dominion and protectorate, precisely its intended role. *Plainfare* was to add a new dimension to the York's service – one of intense usage, relatively short flying distances and repeated take-offs and landings at high all-up-weights.

Plainfare. June 1948 to 12th May 1949.

In 1948 Germany was a nation divided into two parts: East and West Germany; a division that had existed since 1945 and which would continue for decades thereafter. The forces of the Soviet Union occupied the eastern portion of the country, while the western portion was divided amongst the allied nations of the UK,

USA and France. Reflecting the geographical division of Germany was the physical division of Berlin by the same occupying nations. The problem for the occupants of West Berlin, however, was that the city lay approximately 100 miles within the Soviet's sphere, with the latter only grudgingly allowing access to the city via specifically defined road, rail and air corridors. Following a period of heightened tension, the Soviets closed the road and rail links in June 1948, bringing the threat of starvation to the two million or so German residents of West Berlin; only the air corridors were left open. Supplying the citizens and garrison by air alone was doubtless perceived by the Soviet leadership to be inconceivable.

Initially known as Operation *Knicker*, this was the codename which covered the first stages of the Berlin Airlift and was intended to supply West Berlin's garrison only. It commenced on 25th June 1948, (some state 24th or 26th June), and was accompanied by Operation *Carter-Paterson* from 29th June which was the codename applied to supplying the civilian population of the stricken city. On 3rd July 1948 the two were combined to become Operation *Plainfare*, and remained so until the official end of the Airlift on 12th May 1949, although in practice aerial supply continued for considerably longer, and, as history now recalls, the Airlift proved to be remarkably successful.

Throughout the duration of the Airlift, at least 110 individual RAF Yorks were employed on the operation, an entirely impressive number considering that only 203 production Yorks entered military service, a few of which went to the RAE, A&AEE and other institutions and were unavailable for *Plainfare*. Additionally, approximately 30 Yorks had been written-off prior to June 1948, with a further 17 being lost during the course of the Airlift due to accidents often caused by undercarriage or engine failures.

Although the figure of 110 was impressive, the quantity actually employed at any one time was significantly less, reducing further with time as a result of unserviceability and accidents in fulfilling a role for which the York was not totally suited. Although the latter may seem to be an odd or surprising statement, the York had been designed as a long-range freighter accommodating sufficient fuel to complete its task, thus requiring relatively fewer landings in the course of its service life. The aircraft's maximum payload was dictated by the quantity (weight) of fuel required to cover a given distance, so, at journey's end, with much of its fuel expended, the York was that much lighter on landing – thus reducing the stresses borne by airframe, engines and undercarriage, particularly the latter. For the flights to Berlin the near-opposite was true, the distances involved equating to a relatively short hop for the York, dictating a marked increase in the frequency of landings. Equally, although the quantity of fuel carried was of course reduced to suit the distance to be covered, the Yorks were required to carry

maximum payloads, the weight of which, unlike fuel, would not be consumed in flight, thus they were landing at a higher all-up-weight, far more frequently than originally intended. The York's serviceability problems could only be exacerbated by such intensive flying, added to which the heavily laden aircraft often had to negotiate temporary taxyways consisting of pierced-steel-planking, to the detriment of their tyres. Further, to the York went the burden of conveying coal to Berlin, the dust from which was particularly insidious and yet, despite all, they conveyed over 230,000 tons of cargo into the city, more than half of the RAF's total contribution by weight, and representing almost 10% of the West's Airlift total of 2.5 million tons.

On the face of it of course, a contradiction exists here – how could the York contribute so much if it was unsuited for purpose and, apparently, increasingly unreliable? The answer lay with the RAF's policy of instigating a high degree of maintenance to a regular schedule, paying particular attention to the York's undercarriage and brakes for the reasons explained above. Although this reduced the number of Yorks available at any given moment, it ensured a higher degree of reliability; additionally, at specific points in time, Yorks were despatched to civilian contractors for greater in-depth maintenance. Such measures could not eradicate serviceability problems or accidents caused by technical or structural failures, but they did assist in ensuring that the York's problems were contained within satisfactory limits.

In practical terms, the ending of the Berlin Airlift also marked an end for the majority of Yorks in active RAF service which was brought about by two primary considerations. The first was that the Yorks replacement, the Handley Page Hastings was, by late-1949,

G-AGJA, ex-MW103, being towed out of a hangar on January 14th 1944, confirming that its civil registration, allocated on 8th January, had been applied at least two weeks prior to being transferred to BOAC. This York remained with BOAC, until 29th May 1951, when it was bought by the Lancashire Aircraft Corporation Ltd. Whilst with this company G-AGJA received at different times the temporary military serials WW541 and WW508 which were applied for troop-carrying flights. In February 1955 this aircraft was bought by Skyways Ltd. It was withdrawn from use in May 1959 and scrapped during the following August. Both this and the previous image convey an impression of the York's 'box-like' fuselage.
Newark Air Museum

Above and below: Quite apart from VVIP, VIP and first class-equipped variants, the York's *raison d'être* was the long-distance haulage of freight, equipment, troops and supplies as required, which in turn required adequate access to the fuselage's interior for larger loads. Although neither aircraft shown here is identified, the first – showing a jeep – is most likely to be MW105, the first one (the only one?) to be fitted with a detachable, tapered fuselage panel 8ft wide and approximately 6ft high. In this manner, four jeeps could be carried in addition to the York's own lightweight ramp; although, to the author's inexpert eye, the ramp viewed here looks a little too heavy and robust to qualify as 'lightweight'. Later, both freighter and passenger/freighter Yorks were equipped with hinged, double freight doors as seen fitted to York 'O'. The combined passenger/freighter variants could accommodate up to 24 passenger seats in forward compartments with freight and luggage aft; or, when required, the seats could be removed altogether returning the aircraft to a single-role function.
Author's collection

available in quantity, while the second related to the condition of the ex-Airlift Yorks, most of which required extensive refurbishment and repair. Consequently most were withdrawn, overhauled and placed in long-term storage and ultimately scrapped or, for many, sold on to civilian airlines often following periods of four or more years in storage. Despite this, about 25 Yorks were maintained on long-distance route flying from mid-1949 until October 1950, thereafter only a few Yorks remained in service, their numbers dwindling until eventually, the final RAF example - MW295 'Ascalon II ', was flown back to the UK from Singapore in early 1957 and sold.

Surprisingly perhaps, the longest-lived Yorks in active military service proved to be those that had been purchased by France from ex-RAF stocks and operated by the Aeronavale from Le Bourget, France. These were: MW234, MW243 and MW265, which became PA.1, PA.2 and PA.3 respectively; they were delivered in October 1954, (MW243, PA.2), November 1956, (MW234, PA.1) and February 1957, (MW265, PA.3). A fourth York, MW169, was transferred to the French Air Force in June 1945 for the personal use of General de Gaulle, until it was passed on to the Aeronavale to later become PA.4 in 1947. Additionally, and in order to add a whiff of confusion, some sources state that York MW137 was sold to the Aeronavale in June 1956: it too was apparently marked as PA.1. Was this a reporting error, or did MW137 suffer an early accident requiring its replacement by PA.1, MW234 a few months later? Whatever the answer, the remaining French Yorks remained serviceable until 1962, with the suggestion that PA.3 was still flying in mid-1963. Until the end, each retained and displayed its ex-RAF serial number in addition to their respective PA serial numbers.

AVRO YORK SERIAL ALLOCATIONS
All C.I/C.1 unless otherwise stated

Prototypes
LV626 (later became prototype C.II), LV629, LV633, LV639.

Production Yorks
MW100-MW149, MW161-MW210, MW223-MW272, MW284-MW333 = 200 built
PE101-PE108 = 8 built. (PE109-PE129, PE146-PE191, PE224-PE248. 92 cancelled.)
FM400. 1 x Canadian-built York C.III. (Presumably the serials for the 49 Yorks subsequently cancelled would have commenced FM401 to FM449, although the author was unable to confirm this.)

Cancelled orders
TJ720-TJ762, TJ777-TJ807, TJ820-TJ866, TJ881-TJ909. Order placed for 150 Yorks in June 1944; the quantities were successively reduced until the order was cancelled totally in February 1946.

A further order was placed for 60 passenger/freighter Yorks in late-1944, which differed in as much that it formed a combined order for the RAF and BOAC. However, those intended for the RAF were cancelled leaving 25 for BOAC. Nevertheless, the remaining 25 Yorks were allocated the military serials TS789-TS813 inclusive, it being certain that some, though probably not all, were briefly flown wearing their respective military serials and national markings prior to their replacement with civil registrations for service with BOAC.

TZ483-TZ531, TZ547-TZ569. Order for 72 Yorks placed in February 1945; the quantities were successively reduced until cancelled totally in February 1946. (Some sources state that 85 Yorks were ordered with the serial numbers thus extending to TZ582.)

A number of civilian operated Yorks were employed on troop-carrying duties in the 1950s and for this they were required to wear British military serials and national markings. Strictly speaking they fall outside of this titles parameters, however, please refer to the caption on page 89 covering the photograph of York WW579, (G-AGOF, ex-TS808) where a little additional information on this subject has been included.

AVRO YORK:
RAF SQUADRONS AND OTHER UNITS.

SQUADRONS

No.24 Sqn: Already in existence, this Squadron operated Yorks firstly from May 1943 until Oct 1944, and later from July 1946 to Dec 1951. In addition this unit operated Dakotas, Avro Lancastrians, Hastings and other types concurrently with the York. No known Squadron two-letter codes allocated.

No.40 Sqn: Reformed 1st December 1947 with Yorks and disbanded on 15th March 1950. This unit's Yorks were allocated the Squadron two-letter code 'LE'.

No.51 Sqn: Re-equipped with Yorks to replace the Stirling Mk.IV and Mk.V in January 1946, No.51 Squadron was disbanded on 30th October 1950. This unit applied the Squadron two-letter code 'TB' from January 1946 until replaced by 'MH' in early 1950; the code it had previously used in WWII.

No.59 Sqn: Reformed 1st December 1947 with Yorks and disbanded 30th October 1950. This unit's Yorks received the Squadron two-letter code 'BY'.

No.99 Sqn: Reformed on 17th November 1947 with Yorks. Re-equipped with Hastings C.1 and C.2 from August 1949, its last York was gone by September. No known Squadron two-letter codes allocated.

No.206 Sqn: Reformed on 17th November 1947 with Yorks. Disbanded in August 1949. No known Squadron two-letter codes allocated.

No.242 Sqn: Yorks supplemented Stirling Mk.Vs from April 1945, although the former were subsequently withdrawn during July 1945 and replaced with the Stirling Mk.IV. The Squadron then continued to use the Stirlings until Yorks were once again received in December 1945, which completely replacing the Stirlings during January 1946. Re-equipped with the Hastings C.1 from August 1949, the last Yorks had gone by September. This unit used the Squadron two-letter code 'KY'.

No.246 Sqn: Yorks supplemented Halifax IIIs and (later) Liberator IIIs and VIs from December 1944 and remained with the unit until it was disbanded on 16th October 1946 to become No.511 Squadron. No.246 Squadron had used the Squadron two-letter code 'VU'.

No.511 Sqn: Yorks supplemented Dakotas from September 1943 and remained with this unit until it was disbanded on 7th October 1946. Reformed nine days later following the renumbering of No.246 Squadron, the Yorks were retained until withdrawn in August 1949; Hastings being received in September. No known Squadron two-letter codes allocated.

Air Headquarters India Communication Squadron

This Squadron reformed in March 1946, its title being amended to Air Headquarters (Supreme) Communication Squadron in August 1947. Equipped with various types of aircraft, the Squadron appears only to have hosted one York - MW102, Lord Louis Mountbatten's personal aircraft during his tenure as Governor General of India. The Squadron disbanded on 1st December 1947, elements of which then formed the RAF Communication Flight.

Metropolitan Communication Squadron.

Formed on 8th April 1944 from No.510 Squadron which had undertaken communications flying within the UK, a task continued by the newly named unit. Yorks were added to this Squadron from September 1944. The Squadron remained inexistence until 19th July 1948 on which date it became No.31 Squadron equipped with Anson C.12s, C.19s, Proctors and even a Spitfire PR.19, but no Yorks.

FLIGHTS

No.1310 Flight: Reformed on 31st March 1953 as No.1310 (Transport) Flight, this unit was equipped with at least three Yorks in support of the guided weapons trials then being conducted in Australia. The unit was disbanded on 7th December 1953.

No.1359 Flight: Formed on 1st December 1945 as No.1359 (Transport) Flight, or possibly as No.1359 (VIP Flight Transport) Flight it performed duties as Transport Command's VIP Flight until absorbed into No.24 Squadron at the end of June 1946. In addition to Yorks, the Flight also operated four Lancasters. The two-letter code 'ZW' was allocated to this Flight but appears never to have been used.

Governor-General's Flight, Australia.
Formed at Canberra on 4th April 1945, for the use of the Australian Governor-General, it consisted of a York, Avro Anson XII and Percival Proctor IV. The Flight disbanded on 4th June 1947, (see caption for MW140).

RAF Communication Flight
Formed in December 1947 in India. Equipped with at least two Yorks and nine Dakotas it was disbanded on 30th June 1948.

RAF Far East Communications Flight (later Squadron).
Reformed in January 1947 at Singapore, it was tasked to perform communication, transport and VIP flying duties and operated a host of aircraft types including Yorks. The Flight disbanded on 15th October 1947 but reformed the same day as the Far East Communication Squadron, (FECS); this was the unit which hosted both 'Ascalon' and 'Ascalon II' (see caption for LV633). Brought within the control of the Far East Transport Wing in January 1952, the FECS was finally disbanded in February 1959.

VVIP Flight: Formed in December 1944 as a detachment of No.24 Squadron the Flight operated York LV633 'Ascalon' and probably other Yorks as well a least three Douglas C-54 Skymasters at various times during its period of existence. The Flight was disbanded in November 1945.

CONVERSION UNITS

No.1332 CU: Formed in September 1944 as No.1332 (Transport) Heavy Conversion Unit (HCU), to train transport crews using a complement of Stirlings, Liberators, Yorks, Halifaxes and Dakotas at varying times. The Unit was disbanded on 5th January 1948 and became No.241 Operational Conversion Unit (OCU). Having had the two-letter code 'YY' allocated to the HCU, it was retained and used by the OCU.

No.1384 CU: Formed in November 1945 utilizing the personnel from No.6 Lancaster Finishing School which had itself been formed at the beginning of 1945 to train Lancastrian crews for both Transport Command and BOAC. On 1st November the School was renamed No.1384 Heavy (Transport) Conversion

Unit, and received Yorks shortly thereafter. The Unit disbanded on 30th June 1946. It seems likely that Yorks MW108 and MW113 were employed by this Unit, both of which had earlier been transferred to BOAC.

No.241 OCU: Formed on 5th January 1948 from No.1332 HCU, it later merged with No.240 OCU to form No.242 OCU on 16th April 1951. (See caption for York MW149 for further details of his unit).

OTHER UNITS

Yorks are also known to have been allocated to the following units for use in experimental and development programmes. They were: A&AEE; Airborne Forces Experimental Establishment; Air Ministry Servicing Development Unit; Air Transport Tactical Development Unit; RAE; Transport Command Aircrew Examining Unit; Transport Command Development Unit; Transport Command Examining Unit; Tropical Experimental Unit (under the umbrella of A&AEE).

The listing above incorporates those squadrons, flights and other units for which the author has reliable information. It would however be a deception for him to pretend that the list is exhaustive, particularly with regard to 'other units', several more of which must surely have had one or more Yorks attached at various times for varying periods. It is hoped though that the list, as imperfect as it, may prove to be of some benefit to the reader.

An unidentified York, probably seen shortly after completion as, externally at least, it appears to be unfinished. Namely: the fuselage roundel is only three-quarters applied (although its stencilled outline appears on the fuselage access door); a location point only for the port-upper wing roundel is in place, while the starboard wing is devoid of any such marking; the side panel of the starboard-outer engine nacelle is painted black - as if originally intended for a Lancaster perhaps?
Tony Buttler Collection

Above: York MW140 was allocated for use by the Governor-General of Australia, HRH the Duke of Gloucester. His duties would require him to visit all parts of the enormous dominion over which he had authority and clearly therefore air transport was vital. Consequently the 'Governor-General's Flight, Australia' was formed at Canberra on 4th April 1945, (it disbanded on 4th June 1947) and consisted of an Avro Anson XII, Percival Proctor IV NP336, and York MW140. MW140 was first flown on 10th November 1944, its interior being, as to be expected, specially appointed for royal accommodation, and went first to No.246 Squadron in February 1945 in preparation for its delivery flight to Australia, where it arrived on 10th March. It returned to the UK in January 1947 and shortly afterwards went to Langar for 10 months undergoing repairs; thereafter much of its active life was spent with

No.24 Squadron until it entered storage in March 1952. It was sold to a civil airline in September 1954. This undated image post-dates the York's service as the Governor-General of Australia's conveyance.
via Author

Below: York MW140. Whilst serving with the Governor-General's Flight, Australia, MW140 was adorned with the appropriate crest shown here. In addition, this York later had the name 'Endeavour' applied just forward of the crest. As with other VIP Yorks towards the end of the war, MW140 was stripped of paint (assuming it was applied in the first instance) leaving a highly polished bare-metal exterior.
Newark Air Museum

Above: York C.1 MW149, 'YY-H', No.1332 HCU, 1947. First flown on 17th January 1945, this York was operated in turn by No.246 Squadron, No.1332 HCU, No.241 OCU and finally No.59 Squadron. Thereafter MW149 was placed in storage from March 1950, until July 1954, following which it was sold to Dan-Air Ltd and registered G-ANTJ until withdrawn 10 years later. Number 1332 Conversion Unit was formed on 5th September 1945 as No.1332 (Transport) Heavy Conversion Unit at Longtown, Cumberland, to train transport crews initially using Stirlings, Liberators and Yorks, although Dakotas and Skymasters were added later. Having moved location on a number of occasions the unit was renamed No.1332 Heavy Transport Conversion Unit whilst at Dishforth, Yorkshire in May 1947. Disbanded on 5th January 1948, the unit became No.241 OCU at the same location and date to train aircrews for the long-distance transport role for which it was equipped with 18 Yorks plus a quantity of Halifax A.9s, adding Hastings later. Both units, i.e. No.1332 HCU and No.241 OCU retained the same identifying code 'YY', although in the OCU's case these were not apparently applied to their Halifaxes. Number 241 OCU merged with No.240 OCU to form No.242 OCU at Dishforth on 16th April 1951, but by then the York's presence with the unit had ceased; the last having been replaced by Hastings in 1950. Roger Lindsay

Below: Camouflaged York C.1 MW177, 'VU-K', No.246 Squadron seen between 26th February 1946, the date on which this aircraft joined the Squadron and October 1946, the month that this unit was disbanded then reformed as No.511 Squadron. Granted, this is a poor quality photograph, but its inclusion is warranted as images of post-war camouflaged Yorks complete with code letters are not particularly common. The motif below the cockpit appears to be a variation of Transport Command's Motif, artistic variation seemingly varying in application from one unit to another! Following a long period of storage and refurbishment between September 1949 and June 1954, MW177 was sold for civilian use and registered G-ANTH in July 1954; it was finally withdrawn in April 1956. Author's collection

Opposite page top: **Non-camouflaged York C.1 MW187, 'VU-M', No.246 Squadron at Cairo West, Egypt, in late 1945. Transport Command's Motif appears below the cockpit in quite different style to MW177; a Liberator can be seen in the background. Following its Squadron's disbandment, this York was transferred to No.511 Squadron and later to No.59 Squadron in late-1949. Placed in storage during March 1950, it was sold for scrap in late-1953.** Roger Lindsay

Opposite page bottom: **Non-camouflaged York C.1 MW_32, seen at an air display in September 1946. As for its identity, only three serial numbers can stand as contenders: MW132, MW232 or MW332. MW132 was engaged in glider-towing trials at this time, while MW332 was first flown in 1947, leaving MW232 as the best (only) candidate. MW232 had been returned to Avro for repair during August 1946, having suffered damage whilst operating with No.242 Squadron, then based at Oakington, near Cambridge, coded 'KY-M'. It was returned to the Squadron near to the end of August 1946. The placard in front of the York reads 'AVRO YORK Mk C1 FREIGHTER. REPAIRED BY AVRO (illegible) FOR RAF TRANSPORT COMMAND'. Operated later on by No.511 Squadron, it subsequently underwent periods of repair, storage and refurbishment. Placed in long-term storage from June 1951, it was sold to Dan-Air Services Ltd in July 1954 and registered G-ANTK and survives to this day. (See also 'Demobbed' section.)** Newark Air Museum

Above: **York C.1 MW287, 'BY-G', No.59 Squadron, Luqa, Malta. Number 59 Squadron was equipped with Yorks from December 1947 until October 1950, which, for part of that time at least, displayed its individual aircraft codes in a smaller size than its unit code letters. For many RAF Yorks, 1950 represented the year in which a large quantity were entered into storage, never to fly with the RAF again, barring ferry flights from one MU to another, or for refurbishing – as indeed many were. MW287 was no exception, and, as with a number of ex-RAF Yorks, a second career was found flying with civilian airlines or air-freight companies and MW287 was sold to the Canadian company Spartan Air Services in August 1955 and received the civil registration CF-HIP.** Roger Lindsay

OPERATION *PLAINFARE*

The following images were taken during the period of the Berlin Airlift

York C.1 MW145, 'YY-S', No.241 OCU, near RAF Wunstorf, West Germany, on or shortly after 30th July 1949. Although this incident occurred after Operation 'Plainfare' had officially ended, supply flights were continued for several weeks, not least of all because the East German railway system was closed by 'striking' workers. MW145 is seen here following a take-off attempt from Wunstorf on 30th July, during which both port engines lost power and the aircraft swung off the runway. The undercarriage was raised to bring it to a stop with the result seen here; there were no reported injuries. MW145 was struck off charge that same day.
Newark Air Museum

York C.1 MW311, 'TB-C', No.51 Squadron, Abingdon, Oxfordshire, 27th July 1948. Employed in Operation 'Plainfare', MW311 swung on take-off causing the starboard undercarriage to collapse. It was struck off charge the following day. The number '16' seen on the central fin was an Airlift number, a form of fleet number which was a fairly common feature, but not one apparently applied to all of the RAF Yorks involved. via Author

Above: A familiar image of Yorks (with Avro Lancastrians in the far distance) at Gatow, West Berlin, during September 1948. York 'KY-N', is MW267 from No.242 Squadron which, following repairs, joined the Airlift in July 1948, presumably receiving the number '16' vacated by MW311 following the latter's demise on 27th July. MW267 was retained on the Berlin route until August 1949, following which it went into storage and remained there until scrapped in early 1952. via Author

Below: Although supplied without any accompanying information regarding date or location, the RAF lorry registered RAF 37740 offers a clue to the latter as it bears upon its tailboard the word 'Gatow'. In addition it also declares: 'MAX SPEED 25 MPH', 'RIGHT HAND DRIVE NO SIGNALS' and 'BAFO46'. the serial numbers of each of the five Yorks are obscured. via Author

These two images were recieved just prior to going to press and are therefore out of the established sequence.

Above: York MW102 in 1946 or 1947, when in use as Lord Louis Mountbatten's personal aircraft when he was serving as Governor General of India, as witnessed by the circular motif situated below the cockpit. Having sustained serious damage in October 1950, MW102 was struck off charge in December 1950 in Singapore. FAA Museum

Below: York 'VU-G' of No.246 Squadron at an undisclosed location in the Middle East on an unknown date. A Liberator dominates the foreground. FAA Museum

IN QUASI-MILITARY SERVICE

Top and above: Strictly speaking, despite the application of military serials and national markings, these two images are not military Yorks and fall outside of the parameters of this work. They do however warrant a brief explanation if only to add to that inferred in the earlier caption regarding York G-AGJA, (ex-MW103). Civilian-operated Yorks (as well as other civil transports e.g. the Handley Page Hermes), were often temporarily taken on charge by the military to convey British troops to areas such as the Suez Canal Zone and Far East, for which the policy was to apply both military serials and national markings to the aircraft involved. With the York, the serials allocated fell intermittently in the WW, XA, XD, XE, XF, XG and XJ ranges, and it was not unknown for an individual York to receive different military serials on separate occasions; G-AGJA being one. The first image is of York WW579, (G-AGOF, ex-TS808), then owned by the Lancashire Aircraft Corporation Ltd, who acquired it from BOAC in February 1952. They retained it for three years before withdrawing it from use, after which it was presumably scrapped. The second, rather poor quality image, shows York XG897, with its hard to discern serial located just below, and aft of, the fuselage roundel. XG897 was an ex-RAF York C.1 serialled MW326 which, following two years in storage, was sold to Surrey Flying Services Ltd in January 1952, receiving the civil registration G-AMRJ shortly afterwards. It was then operated by Air Charter Ltd, whose logo 'ACL' appears behind the cockpit and was normally employed on flights into West Berlin. G-AMRJ was sold to a Lebanese company in July 1955. Both author's collection

IN FRENCH NAVAL SERVICE

Above: York C.1, PA.1, MW234 seen at an undisclosed location in 1960, with PA.3 beyond. As can be seen, the original RAF serial number was retained on the fuselage, while that on PA.3 was situated beneath the tailplane. Newark Air Museum

Below: York C.1, PA.3, MW265, seen at Le Bourget in June 1963 and presumably close to the end of its active life. By this time the ex-RAF serial number, MW265, had been relocated to the vertical fin and the diameter of the national markings reduced significantly. A Lancaster's rear turret and part of its tailplane can just be identified directly in front of PA.3's nose. Newark Air Museum

DEMOBBED

Above: **York G-AMUU, ex-MW183. First flown on 2nd June 1945,** MW183 was operated by No.511 Squadron and later with No.246 Squadron coded 'VU-R', before returning to No.511 Squadron in October 1946, for two months. Thereafter, apart from participating in the Berlin Airlift, it remained either in storage or undergoing refurbishment. By 22nd September 1952, this aircraft had been sold to Air Charter Ltd and registered as G-AMUU. By January 1956 it was being operated by Hunting-Clan Air Transport and was withdrawn from use in 1959 and scrapped at Heathrow. The unmistakable nose of a Boeing Stratocruiser is visible behind the hangar door.
Newark Air Museum

Below: **York G-ANTI, ex-MW143, seen at Lasham, Hampshire 21st April** 1963, minus its engines. Having been operated by several RAF squadrons this York was placed in storage in October 1950, remaining there until sold to Dan-Air Services Ltd in mid-1954, and registered G-ANTI. It remained with that company until its official permanent withdrawal from use on 3rd September 1964. *Newark Air Museum*

Top: York G-ANTJ, ex-MW149 (see separate caption), also at Lasham, on 21st April 1963, minus two of its engines. Were these two airframes retained as a source of spares for the last Yorks in revenue earning service – a few of which lingered on into 1963? Despite its condition and appearance, it too was not officially withdrawn from service until 3rd September 1964, the year that Dan-Air's last York, G-ANTK, made its last flight in company service during April, a week prior to flying to Lasham to be stored on the last day of that month – its last flight. The very last York to fly, Skyway's G-AGNV has been mentioned elsewhere in this book. Newark Air Museum

Above: This anonymous-looking, whitewashed York is in fact G-ANTK, ex-MW232 (see separate caption). Seen at Lasham post-October 1964, it is just possible to read the registration applied to the underside of its port wing. Somehow, this aircraft survived the attentions of the scrap man and today, owned by the Duxford Aviation Society and fully restored in Dan-Air's livery, it may be seen on display inside the Airspace Hangar at Duxford Aerodrome, Cambridgeshire. Newark Air Museum

APPENDIX 1: *TIGER FORCE*

Often referred to in this volume, Appendix 1 is provided to supply a more detailed background to 'Tiger Force', the existence of which otherwise falls outside the scope of this volume, other than for its post-war legacy of FE standard Lancasters and the Lincoln bomber. Tiger Force's details appear here so as not to interfere with the main body of text.

As the war against Germany appeared to be nearing an end, the RAF was engaged in considering further contributions that it could make towards the war against Japan, and an initial plan was formulated for Bomber Command to send three bomber groups to the Pacific to join with the USAAF in their strategic bombing campaign against the Japanese home islands. These groups would form the basis of 'Tiger Force' which was officially established on the 24th February 1945, under the command of Air Vice Marshal Sir Hugh Lloyd KBE, CB. The plan was for Tiger Force to be based on recently captured islands in the Pacific but when the Americans were approached with the idea they were concerned about the large size of the force as there was a shortage of suitable airfields in the area. This resulted in the original force being trimmed back and reorganised as 'Tiger Force (revised)'.

Instead of three groups, the Force was cut to two, and was to comprise 19 bomber squadrons each equipped with 20 aircraft. Further, six Mosquito fighter-escort squadrons were also included as well as additional units operating in the Photo Reconnaissance, Meteorological Reconnaissance, Air Sea Rescue and Transport roles. Also, as they became available, both the Hawker Tempest F.II and DH Hornet F.1 were expected to supplement or replace existing fighters within the Force. It was intended that all of the bomber squadrons were to have been equipped with the Lincoln then being developed by Avro but, due to engine development problems, not nearly enough of these were available dictating that Tiger Force would have to operate using a mixed complement of Lancaster and Lincoln heavy bombers instead. Further cutbacks occurred when all six fighter-escort squadrons were excluded following the discovery that the wooden Mosquito was susceptible to the heat and humidity of tropical conditions, which could result in catastrophic structural weaknesses; yet this ban did not prevent the retention of other Mosquitos required for the pathfinder and reconnaissance roles!

The Australian, Canadian and New Zealand governments each wanted their own air forces to participate, and so squadrons from these countries, which were already serving in Bomber Command, were to be included with the Canadians volunteering to provide the majority of its complement of No.6 (RCAF) Group.

NO.5 GROUP

No.551 Wing

No.83 Sqn	Lancaster B.I(FE)
No.97 Sqn	Lancaster B.I(FE)
No.627 (Pathfinder Sqn)	Mosquito B.35

No.552 Wing

No.106 Sqn	Lancaster B.I(FE)
No.467 (RAAF) Sqn	Lancaster B.I(FE)
No.544 (Met) Sqn	Mosquito PR.34

No.553 Wing

No.57 Sqn	Lincoln B.II
No.460 (RAAF) Sqn	Lincoln B.II

No.554 Wing

No.75 (RNZAF) Sqn	Lancaster B.I(FE)
No.207 Sqn	Lancaster B.I(FE)

Special Missions Wing

No.9 Sqn	Lancaster B.VII(FE)
No.617 Sqn	Lancaster B.VII(FE)

NO.6 (RCAF) GROUP

No.661 Wing

No.431 RCAF Sqn	Lancaster B.X(FE)
No.434 RCAF Sqn	Lancaster B.X(FE)

No.662 Wing

No.419 RCAF Sqn	Lancaster B.X(FE)
No.428 RCAF Sqn	Lancaster B.X(FE)

No.663 Wing

No.420 RCAF Sqn	Lancaster B.X(FE)
No.425 RCAF Sqn	Lancaster B.X(FE)

No.664 Wing

No.405 RCAF Sqn	Lincoln B.XV Canadian-built Lincoln. FM300 was the only example completed.
No.408 RCAF Sqn	Lincoln B.XV

OTHER UNITS

No.179 ASR Sqn	Lancaster ASR.III Complement of 10 x ASR.IIIs & 10 x Catalinas
No.279 ASR Sqn	Lancaster ASR.III Complement of 10 x ASR.IIIs & 10 x Catalinas

Communications Flight

	Auster V and Beech Expeditor II

Force Reserve

No.49 Sqn	Lancaster B.I(FE)
No.189 Sqn	Lancaster B.I(FE)

By 15th August 1945, the intended Order of Battle stood as indicated in the accompanying list, with a projected deployment date of September-November 1945, in readiness for offensive operations to commence in 1946.

Following VE Day, those Canadian units of No.6 (RCAF) Group equipped with (Canadian-built) Lancaster B.Xs, left the UK and returned to Canada to prepare for their deployment to the Pacific. It was hoped that as many squadrons as possible would re-equip with the Lincoln B.XV to be produced by 'Victory Aircraft' of Malton, Toronto; but, in case of production delays, their Lancaster B.Xs were to be brought up to the same FE standard as British Lancasters and used either operationally or to act as reserves. In the event only one Lincoln B.XV was completed.

The whole of *Tiger Force* was to have staged through Canada on its way to the Far East. However, for the time being, those units remaining in the UK were grouped in Lincolnshire and East Anglia from where they began a rigorous training regime – by both day and night. In these, Lancaster and Lincoln crews conducted extra long range navigational and bombing exercises in order to test fuel consumption and to acclimatise themselves to flying for long periods over the featureless sea. Orders were also passed specifying that nobody was expected to fly a third tour of operations whilst with *Tiger Force*. Anyone who was over halfway through their second tour by VE Day had to be posted out and exchanged for eligible aircrew from non-*Tiger Force* units. This affected large numbers of personnel and most squadrons.

Changes also had to be made to the aircraft that would equip *Tiger Force* as the Lancaster was not known for its ability to operate in hot and dusty tropical conditions where its in-line liquid-cooled Merlin engines had a tendency to rapidly boil if ground-run for too long. To try and remedy this problem, all of the Lancasters intended for Tiger Force received a number of modifications, either on the production line or at No.32 MU at St Athan, Glamorgan, and the decision was taken to use only Rolls-Royce built Merlin-powered Lancaster B.Is and B.VIIs in order to avoid any future shortage of Packard-built Merlin engines.

The principal modification was the fitting of tropicalised Merlin 24 engines which could better cope with heat and dust, in addition the latest electrical aids were also fitted such as Gee Mk.III, Rebecca Mk.II, Loran Mk.I, and H2S Mk.IIG whilst American SCR-522 radios were to be incorporated at a later date too. All bomber versions of the Lancaster bound for *Tiger Force* also received FN.82 rear turrets which were armed with a pair of .5in Browning machine guns. Once modified, the Lancasters received the added suffix (FE) for Far East and, as little or no fighter threat was expected in the Pacific, their upper surfaces and sides were painted in an overall white finish which was better able to reflect heat off the airframe and keep the interior and wing mounted fuel tanks cooler. Their under surfaces were painted anti-searchlight black to help counter ground based defences during nocturnal operations over Japan. All FE modified Lancasters had provision for a 400 gallon auxiliary fuel tank in the rear of the bomb bay, but to counter this added weight the mid-upper turret was to be removed. Under these conditions, a maximum range of 3,180 miles could be achieved whilst carrying a full fuel load of 2,554 gallons, and a reduced bomb load of 7,000lbs. The maximum bomb load of FE standard Lancasters was slightly higher at 10,000lb which would normally consist of a 4,000lb 'Cookie' and six 1,000lb bombs, although the Special Missions Wing Lancasters operated by Nos.9 and 617 Squadrons were capable of carrying 12,000lb Tallboy deep penetration bombs if required. However this could only be achieved by using specially up-rated engines and air-to-air refuelling as the Lancaster's fuel tanks would have to be replenished following take off for long-range operations in order to keep its take off weight within limits.

In fact the original intention was for the whole of Tiger Force to make use of the air-to-air refuelling methods devised and pioneered by Sir Alan Cobham's Flight Refuelling Ltd and at the early planning stages when Tiger Force was expected to be an all Lincoln force comprising of at least 500 aircraft it was envisaged that an equal number of Lancaster's would act as their tankers. Another approach toward extending the range of bombers was to equip a pair of experimental Lancasters (SW244 and HK541) with huge dorsal 'saddle tanks' and they flew a number of long range proving flights but the idea never progressed any further because of the inherent fire hazard.

Even at a scaled-down two group level, *Tiger Force* was still an impressive formation which was to have had a complement of 66,305 personnel with over 3,000 vehicles to support the operations of around 500 aircraft. By June 1945 the first RAF personnel had arrived on Okinawa to set up an air depot at Naha, but once in theatre they found that they were vying for facilities against the USAAF's 8th Air Force which was also due to arrive imminently, having returned to the USA after VE Day to re-equip with B-29's.

It was obvious that despite promises to the contrary there were just not enough bases and facilities available on Okinawa to accommodate both of these large bomber forces as well as the units already based there so contingency plans were made for Tiger Force to be split. The majority of squadrons would still be based on Okinawa, although the remainder was to be reallocated to South East Asia Command (SEAC), where they would be based along the eastern coast of India to operate in support of Allied forces in Malaya. With this in mind some of the squadrons began to retrain for short notice tactical bombing in support of the Army.

All preparations were of course halted by the atomic bombs of August 1945 and *Tiger Force* was disbanded on the 31st October 1945, as were many of its component squadrons.

APPENDIX 2: **LANCASTER OPERATIONS FROM PALESTINE**

The contents of this appendix might be viewed by some as being merely incidental to the Lancaster's history, hence its separation from the main body of text. Whether this is so is a question best left to the reader to answer. However, the period of operations relating to Palestine did provide maritime Lancasters with what was arguably their most intensive period of use between 1945 and 1950.

For centuries conflict has existed between the Arab and Jewish Peoples of the Middle East, none less so than in a country which, until 1948, was known as Palestine. During the years of the British Mandate which followed the overthrow of the Ottoman Empire at the end of WW1, British authorities had sought to maintain a peaceful co-existence between these two communities by displaying equanimity to both sides. However, for the British in the post-WWII era, the financial burden of maintaining over 100,000 military personnel (from all three services) in Palestine was too great. Additionally, British public opinion increasingly demanded an end to the Mandate and in early 1947 the British Government announced their desire to terminate it. The United Nations General Assembly was thus requested to make recommendations regarding the future of the country, for which, Britain would remain responsible until the mandate's termination – set for 15th May 1948.

Count Folke Bernadotte of the United Nations announced a resolution stating that from that date the territory would be partitioned between both Arab and Jew in order to create a new Jewish homeland. This created a furore amongst the Arab population, which was already concerned about the large influx of European Jews into Palestine following WWII; they now feared that an even greater wave of Jewish immigration was to follow. In order to ease Arab fears and prevent any further illegal (to use the contemporary phrase) Jewish immigrants from entering the country, British authorities decided to apply strict immigration controls. This effectively meant intercepting those ships which were conveying Jewish immigrants, turn them, and so prevent them from reaching Palestine; thus the blockade of the Palestinian coastline began, to which was applied the name Operation *Sunburn* (later Operation *Bobcat*).

To implement the blockade, RAF Lancasters were required to mount constant patrols in the central and eastern Mediterranean, whilst the Royal Navy deployed destroyers and other surface vessels which would stop and board those vessels discovered by RAF patrols. If ships were found to be carrying illegal Jewish immigrants, they were to be escorted into port and the immigrants interned in camps created for this purpose in Cyprus.

Unsurprisingly, such actions incensed the Jewish population in Palestine. Undercover Jewish movements began a terrorist campaign against the British which commenced with the murder of British servicemen in the street, many of whom, by bitter irony, had helped liberate Jews from German concentration camps scarcely a year earlier. This escalated into an almost daily series of shootings and bombings culminating in an attack on 22nd July 1946, against the British Military HQ based within the King David Hotel, Jerusalem; 91 people were killed with 46 more injured. It was to be the deadliest attack on British personnel during the period of the mandate. In an effort to disrupt the successful coastal blockade operations, the RAF Control Radar Station at Mount Carmel had earlier (20th February 1946) been bombed, although probably the boldest series of bombings occurred five days later when the RAF airfields at Qastina, Petah Tigya and Lydda were attacked in which 11 Halifax A.7s, two Ansons and seven Spitfire FR.18s were totally destroyed.

In order to bolster the Middle East-based Lancaster units, Coastal Command Lancasters began to deploy from the UK on a regular basis too, usually sending four aircraft at a time on what came to be known as *Bobcat* detachments; the first unit to do so was No.210 Squadron in August 1947. Additionally, Halifax A.7s and A.9s from both No.620 Squadron (later to become No.113 Squadron) at Aqir, plus No.644 Squadron (later No.47 Squadron) based at Qastina. Palestine, also undertook maritime patrols when their principal duties in support of the British 6th Airborne Division (part of the British Army garrison) allowed. Ultimately as the troubles worsened, the paratroopers had less time to devote to airborne training and eventually became unavailable for airborne operations at all, so the Halifaxes were withdrawn from the area.

The captains of the blockade running vessels, specially chartered and often laden with hundreds of hopeful Jews, preferred to approach the Palestinian coast under the cover of darkness, so requiring the RN (including the FAA if aircraft carriers were available) and RAF to mount patrols through the night. When a Lancaster located a suspected blockade runner, using its less than adequate H2S radar they would inform the nearest Royal Navy vessel by radio and guide it to the correct position. The aircraft would then continue to circle the ship until the intercepting warship could send a boarding party to inspect the vessel, often conducted under the illumination of flares dropped by the Lancaster.

Despite their undoubted professionalism in the air, the most outstanding act carried out by a member of the Lancaster squadrons in Palestine actually took place on the ground. On the night of the 28th March 1947, Lancaster ASR.3, RF323, RL-C of No.38 Squadron, was being refuelled at Ein Shemer when a fire broke out which engulfed the refuelling bowser and spread to the nose and cockpit of the aircraft itself. As all of the Lancasters on Ein Shemer's flight-line were parked in a row, the fire placed about 20 other aircraft in jeopardy. The fire in the burning Lancaster was so intense that it could not be immediately extinguished; however, the NCO in charge of the refuelling party – Sgt J A Beckett – ensured the survival of the other aircraft by getting into the cab of the blazing bowser and driving it 400 yards into a safe area before it could explode. Sadly he suffered such extensive burns to his head, face and body that he died of his injuries on 12th April 1947. He was posthumously awarded the George Cross for his bravery.

By the start of 1948, and with the termination of their mandate drawing closer, the British began to withdraw from Palestine and the Lancasters of both Nos.37 and 38 Squadrons were redeployed to Luqa. A detachment of nine Lancasters remained behind however, until almost the very end, at Ramat David, Palestine, which by then was the sole remaining RAF airfield in the theatre and which they shared with the Spitfire FR.18s of Nos.32 and 208 Squadrons. On or about 23rd May 1948, the RAF departed the airfield,

by which date 223 British service personnel had been killed and nearly 480 injured whilst policing Palestine since 1945.

From the start of the joint RAF/RN Blockade in 1946 until the end in May 1948, at least 47 blockade running vessels had been intercepted and over 60,000 Jewish immigrants interned in Cyprus, yet this effort had only staved off the inevitable. After the British withdrew from Palestine the interned Jews were released and without a blockade to prevent them, they continued to their original destination alongside tens of thousands more Jewish immigrants. The United Nations resolution to partition the territory between Arabs and Jews was never realised and the new Jewish state of Israel was created.

Once re-established at Luqa, both Nos.37 and 38 Squadrons began to slowly re-equip with Lancaster GR.3s which they operated into the 1950s, returning to the work which, but for geography and weather conditions, typified the work which Coastal Command's Lancaster squadrons conducted from UK bases – namely search and patrol.

Received just prior to this volume being printed, this image provides a partial view of Lancaster B.7(FE), NX756, 'WS-C' from No.9 Squadron, undergoing a fuel tank change in either the Middle or Far East, presumably while either on route to, or returning from India; a Liberator stands in the foreground. By late-April 1946, NX756 was lodged with No.20 MU prior to serving in turn with the EFS, EAAS and RAFFC; it was struck off charge in September 1950.
FAA Museum

Above and below: **Avro York 'LV633 *Ascalon'*.** Having been allocated the military serial TS798, this York received the civil registration G-AGNV on 20th August 1945 and was operated first by BOAC and later by Skyways Ltd, until officially withdrawn from use in May 1964 and stored. Thereafter it entered into preservation and today, as earlier related, it resides within the National Cold War Exhibition as 'MW100'. In the interim, G-AGNV flew one more time, becoming the last York anywhere to do so when it was flown to Staverton Airport, Gloucestershire, in October 1964 to join the Skyfame Museum. Whilst there it was repainted to represent 'LV633 *Ascalon'*. These two images reveal that in order to enhance '*Ascalon'*'s' appearance, 'square' windows had seemingly been let into the fuselage, although slight scrutiny reveals that several of the original circular windows had been over-painted totally, with others partially so, in order make them appear square. If nothing else, these images give an impression of how a camouflaged wartime or early post-war York might have appeared with the exception of the black under surfaces which, apparently, was unique to the original LV633. No date was supplied with these images, although they were obviously taken at different times. In May 1972, this aircraft was bought by the RAF Museum to later emerge as 'MW100'. Both Author's collection

Left: **York C.1 MW251, 'KY-C' No.242 Squadron, Oakington, 1946.** Delivered to this unit in March 1946, this York was later coded 'KY-J'. In September 1947, MW251 was transferred to No.511 Squadron coded 'CAW' on its nose. It went into storage in October 1949 and was sold for scrap in May 1955. Newark Air Museum

**Lancaster B.7(FE)
NX678, 'WS-S',
No.9 Squadron,
Bomber Command,
circa early 1946.**

This Lancaster was painted
in the Far East white and
black colour scheme to
which a black anti-glare
panel was painted in front
of the cockpit; not a
particularly common
feature on FE Lancasters.
Further details and a
photograph of NX678
appear on page 14.

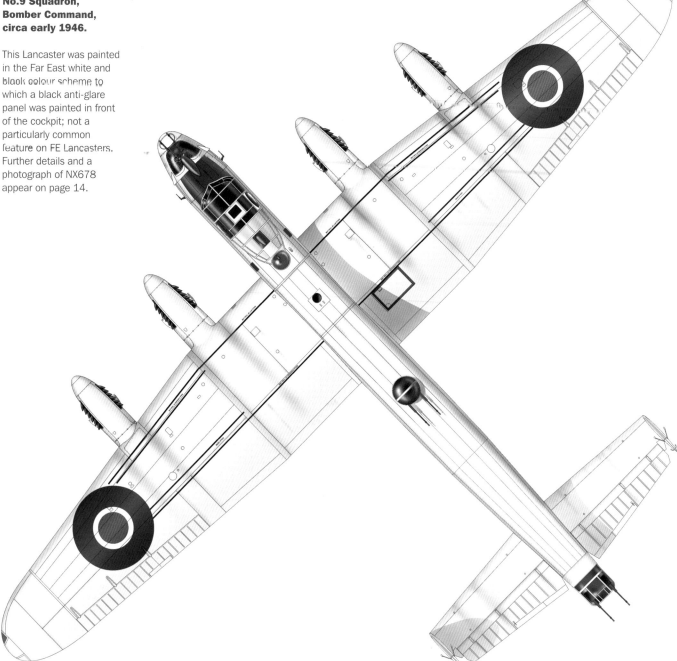

Although the H2S radome appears to be black it
was in reality opaque. See photograph on page 14.

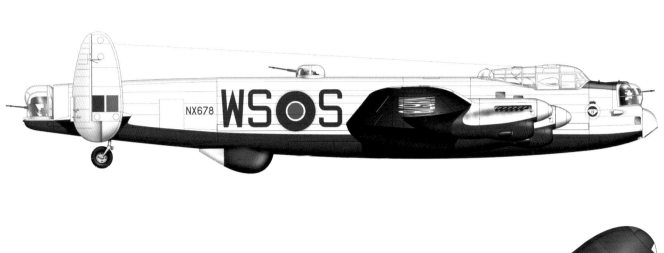

**Lancaster B.7(FE)
NX739. Fighter
Command (see image
and caption on page 44),
circa 1950.**

Shown with all turrets in
place, NX739 was used as
an official air-to-air
photography platform for
much of its life and, at some
point, received the Medium
Sea Grey and black colour
scheme with high fuselage
demarcation line as
depicted here. Very few
Lancasters appeared in this
scheme which was more
commonly associated with
the Lincoln. At a later stage
both the dorsal turret and
H2S dome were removed.
Further details and
photographs of NX739
appear on page 44 and 45.

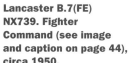

**Lancaster ASR.3
RF314, 'K7-LJ',
No.236 OCU,
Coastal Command,
1947/1948.**

RF314's camouflage
consisted of an Extra
Dark Sea Grey and Slate
Grey disruptive scheme
applied to its sides and
upper surfaces, with Sky
lower surfaces. Further
details and a photograph
of RF314 appear on
page 61.

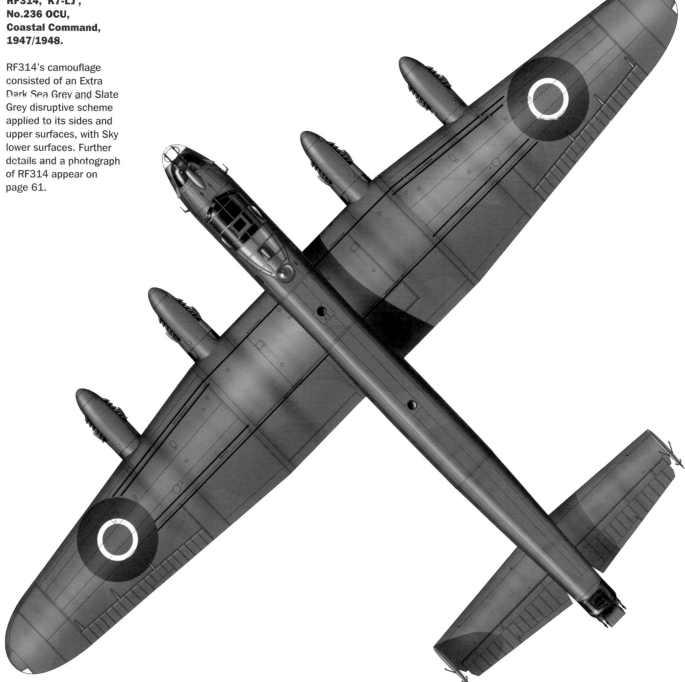

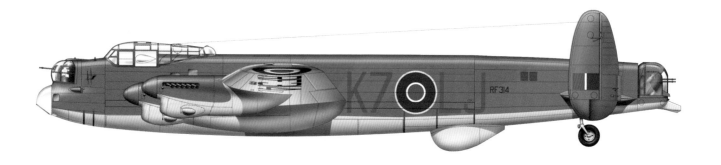

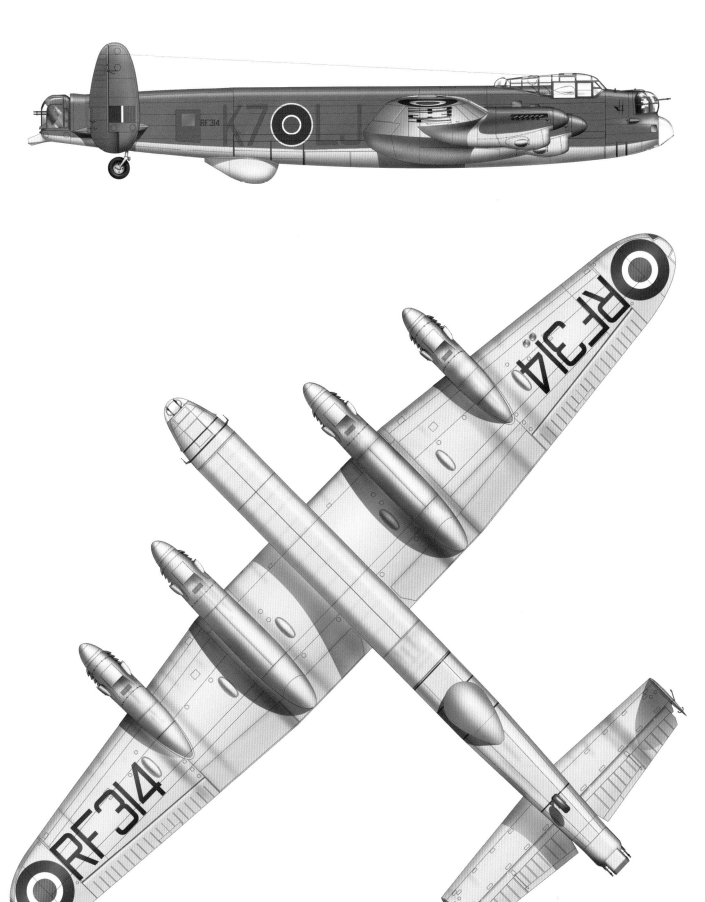

Lincoln B.2 RF472, 'HW-B', No.100 Squadron, Bomber Command.

Depicted as RF472 appeared circa 1947, with only the dorsal turret guns fitted. The disruptive camouflage applied to the upper surfaces consisted of Dark Green and Dark Earth. Further details and a photograph of RF472 appear on page 34.

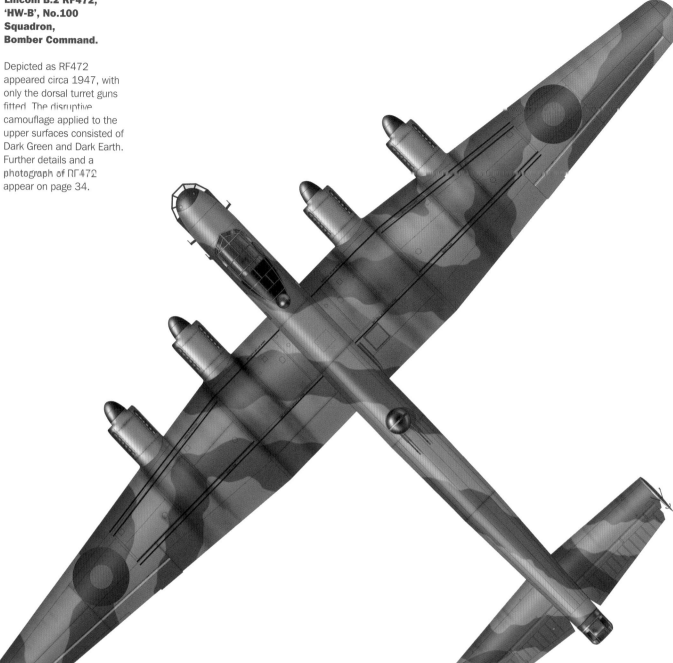

Lincoln B.2 RF523, 'THOR II ', Empire Air Armament School, 1946-1948.

Other than a black anti-glare panel in front of the cockpit and four red propeller-spinner covers, RF523 was unpainted. The apparent lack of any fuselage serials is explained by the fact that they had been moved further aft than was usual and, as here, they were often obscured by the tail fins. Further details and photographs of RF523 appear on page 41.

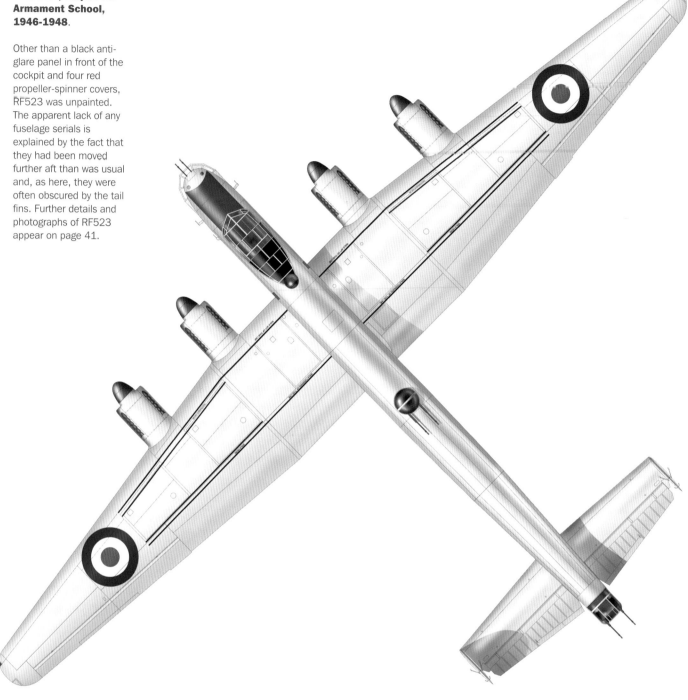

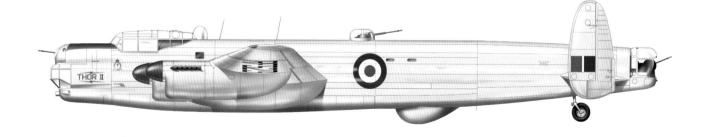

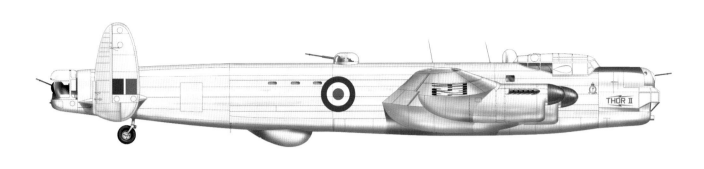

Lincoln B.2 RF532, 'LS-D', No.15 Squadron, Bomber Command, 1947.

RF532 was finished in the post-war bomber scheme which comprised of Medium Sea Grey upper surfaces, black lower surfaces with a high fuselage demarcation line. Wartime national markings were retained at this time. Further details and a photograph of RF532 appears on page 27.

York C.1 MW251, 'KY-C', No.242 Squadron, Transport Command, 1946.

MW251 was either unpainted or, was painted Aluminium overall. Further details and a photograph of MW251 appear on page 97.

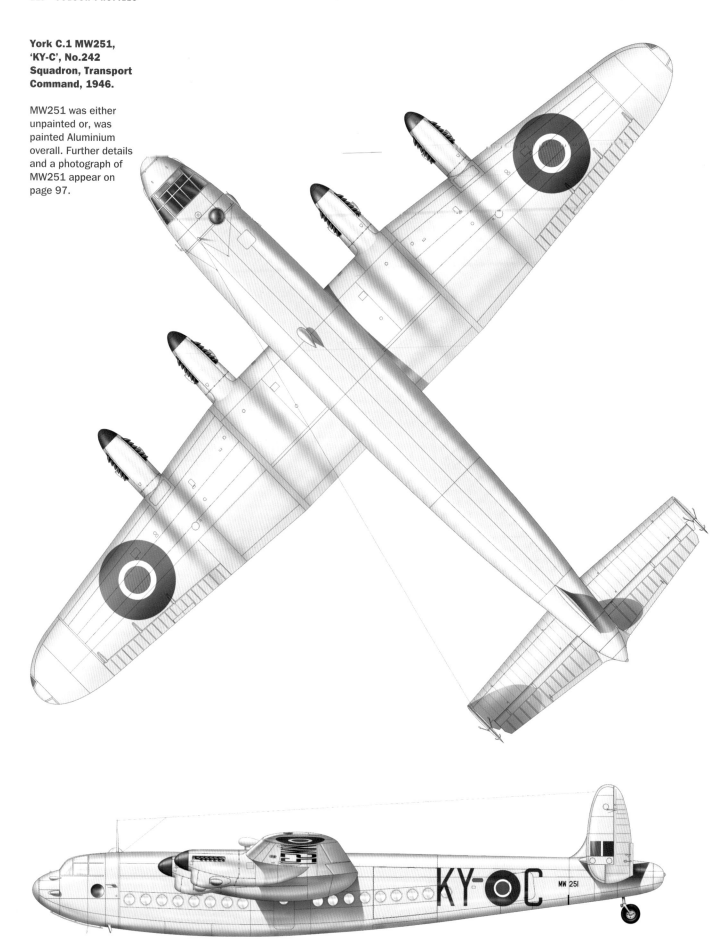

BIBLIOGRAPHY

Action Stations Revisited. No.1 Eastern England: MJF Bowyer; *Crecy Publishing Ltd, 2000.*
Aircraft of the Royal Air Force since 1918: O Thetford; *Putnam & Company Limited, 1976.*
Air Wars and Aircraft 1945 to Present: V Flintham; *Arms and Armour Press, 1989.*
Avro Aircraft since 1908: AJ Jackson; *Putnam & Company Limited, 1990.*
Avro Lancaster, The: FK Mason; *Aston Publications Ltd, 1989.*
Avro Lancaster, The Definitive Record: H Holmes; *Airlife Publishing Ltd, 2001.*
Avro Manchester. The Legend Behind the Lancaster: R Kirby; *Midland Publishing Ltd, 1995.*
British Military Aircraft Serials 1878-1987: B Robertson; *Midland Counties Publications, 1987.*
Broken Wings, Post-War RAF Accidents: JJ Halley; *Air-Britain (Historians) Ltd, 1999.*
Bomber Squadrons of the RAF and their aircraft: P Moyes; *Macdonald and Jane's (Publishers) Limited, 1976.*
Bombs Gone. ... British air-dropped weapons from 1912: JA MacBean; *Patrick Stephens Limited, 1990.*
Britain's Military Aircraft in Colour 1960-1970: M Derry; *Crecy Publishing Ltd, 2010.*
British Military Aviation, 1960s In Colour No.1: M Derry; *Dalrymple & Verdun Publishing, 2007.*
British Piston Aero-Engines and Their Aircraft: A Lumsden; *Airlife Publishing Ltd, 1997.*
Category Five, RAF Aircraft Losses 1954-2009: C Cummings; *Nimbus Publishing, 2009.*
Churchill goes to war: Winston's Wartime Journeys: B Lavery; *Conway, Anova Books, 2008.*
Coastal Support and Special Squadrons of the RAF: JDR Rawlings; *Jane's Publishing company Limited, 1982.*
Cold War Years, The: T Mason; *Hikoki Publications Ltd, 2001.*
Combat Codes...since 1938: V Flintham, A Thomas; *Airlife Publishing Ltd, 2003.*
De Havilland Hornet & Sea Hornet: T Buttler, D Collins, M Derry; *Dalrymple & Verdun Publishing, 2010.*
Final Landings, RAF Aircraft and Combat Losses 1946-1949: C Cummings; *Nimbus Publishing.*
Fleet Air Arm Aircraft, 1939 to 1945: R Sturtivant, M Burrow: *Air-Britain (Historians) Ltd, 1995.*
Fly Navy, Aircraft of the Fleet Air Arm since 1945: R Williams; *Airlife Publishing Ltd, 1989.*
Flying Training And Support Units: R Sturtivant, J Hamlin; *Air-Britain (Historians) Ltd, 2007.*
Flying Units of the RAF: A Lake; *Airlife Publishing Ltd, 1999.*
Forgotten Bombers of the RAF: K Wixey; *Arms And Armour Press, 1997.*
Gloster Meteor (Aerofax): T Buttler, P Butler; *Midland Publishing Ltd, 2006.*
Handley page Halifax, The: KA Merrick; *Aston Publications Ltd, 1990.*
Hastings, Handley Pages Post-War Transport Aircraft: T Senior; *Dalrymple & Verdun Publishing, 2008.*
High Stakes, Britain's Air Arms In Action 1945-1990: V Flintham; *Pen & Sword Books Ltd, 2009.*
Lancaster File, The: JJ Halley; *Air-Britain (Historians) Ltd, 1985.*
Lancaster in action, Squadron Signal No.1052: RSG Mackay; *Squadron Signal Publications, Inc, 1982.*
Lancaster - The Story Of A Famous Bomber: B Robertson: *Harleyford Publications, 1972.*
Lincoln at War 1944-1966: M Garbett and B Goulding; *Ian Allan Ltd, 1979.*
Last Take-Off, RAF Aircraft Losses 1950-1953: C Cummings; *Nimbus Publishing.*
RAF Squadrons: CG Jefford; *Airlife Publishing Ltd, 1988.*
RAF Bomber Command Losses...1945, (plus other years): WR Chorley; *Midland Publishing Ltd, 1998.*
Royal Air Force Aircraft serial monographs (various). *Air-Britain (Historians) Ltd*
Secret Years, The: T Mason; *Hikoki Publications Ltd, 1998.*
Stirling Story, The: MJF Bowyer; *Crecy Publishing Ltd, 2001.*
Source Book of the RAF, The: K Delve; *Airlife Publishing Ltd, 1994.*
Squadrons of the Fleet Air Arm: R Sturtivant, T Balance; *Air-Britain (Historians) Ltd, 1994.*
Squadrons of the RAF and Commonwealth 1918-1988, The; JJ Halley; *Air-Britain (Historians) Ltd, 1988.*
Under B conditions: DS Revell, PH Butler; *Merseyside Aviation Society Publications, 1978.*
Wrecks & Relics, 21st Edition: K Ellis; *Crecy Publishing Ltd, 2008.*
Wrecks & Relics, The Album: K Ellis; *Midland Publishing, 2003.*

ABBREVIATIONS

A&AEE	Aeroplane & Armament Experimental Establishment
AFS	Advanced Flying School
ASR	Air-sea rescue
ASV	Air-to-surface vessel (radar)
ANS	Air Navigation School
APDU	Air Photographic Development Unit
AST	Air Service Training
ASWDU	Air-Sea Warfare Development Unit
BBU	Bomb Ballistics Unit
BCBS	Bomber Command Bombing School
BOAC	British Overseas Aircraft Corporation
CAW	College of Air Warfare
CCGS	Coastal Command Gunnery School
CGS	Central Gunnery School
CN&CS	Central Navigation and Control School
CNS	Central Navigation school
CPE	Central Photographic Establishment
CSE	Central Signals Establishment
EAAS	Empire Air Armament School
EANS	Empire Air Navigation School
EFS	Empire Flying School
FEAF	Far East Air Force
FRL	Flight Refuelling Ltd
GR	general reconnaissance
H2S	An air-to-ground radar system
HCU	Heavy Conversion Unit
JASS	Joint Anti-Submarine School
LTEF	Lincoln Theseus Experimental Flight
MAP	Ministry of Aircraft Production (fully merged into MoS in 1946)
MCS	Metropolitan Communications Squadron
MoS	Ministry of Supply
MR	Maritime reconnaissance
MU	Maintenance Unit
OCU	Operational Conversion Unit
OTU	Operational Training Unit
PR	Photographic Reconnaissance
RAAF	Royal Australian Air Force
RAE	Royal Aircraft Establishment
RAFFC	RAF Flying College
RCAF	Royal Canadian Air Force
RWE	Radio Warfare Establishment
SMR	School of Maritime Reconnaissance
SoATC	School of Air Traffic Control
SOC	struck off charge